A History of the Chinese in the West: 1848-1880.

George R. Mead

E-Cat Worlds Press

Comments and questions? –> gmead01@gmail.com

A History of the Chinese in the West: 1848-1880.

Copyright 2011, 2012 by George R. Mead

LCCN 2011930457

Mead, George R.
A History of the Chinese in the West: 1848-1880./
George R. Mead.
 ISBN-13 978-0-9817446-6-7
          1. History. I. Title. II. Series.

E-Cat Worlds established its publishing program as a reaction to the large commercial publishing houses currently dominating the book industry and the smaller intellectual clones. It is interested in publishing works of fiction and non-fiction that are often deemed insufficiently profitable or commercial or that are not necessarily reflective of literary trends and fads.

E-Cat Worlds, 57744 Foothill Road, La Grande OR 97850
www.ecatworldspress.com
SAN 255-6383

In the middle of nowhere - Creativity.

First Edition, 2011
Revised 2012
Printed in the United States of America

From Grandeville.

Portal
Lair
Search
Not Again
And Again.
Magiwitch
Rebirth
Offspring
Holiday
Treasure
E'Nilt
Braidna

A Tale of The Feyra

Jonathon and Dee
Dee Of The Fontala
Dee and The People

Nonfiction

A History of Union County
The Ethnobotany of the California Indians
A History of the Chinese in the West: 1848-1880

He who learns but does not think, is lost.

He who thinks but does not learn, is in great danger.

Confucius

Table of Contents

Introduction

The Chinese were involved in the history of the West Coast of the United States from its very early development. They began to enter the United States in 1848, and afterwards, attracted by the gold rush which had begun in California.

As the gold discoveries were found further and further to the north, eventually up into Canada, the Chinese appeared along with all the others who were following the gold from discovery to discovery.

The first Chinese entering the United States were primarily involved in the gold mining activities. But, over time, the Chinese entering the U.S. became engaged in many other occupations as well.

This is a history of that invisible population. They were invisible in the sense that there was very little mention of them in the media of the times other than in derogatory terms. As we shall see, the Chinese were involved in much of the development of the West Coast in a number of occupations. Yet, today, we hardly see any mention of them, or acknowledgment of them, in the many usual histories of the period of time at which we are about to look. Hence, the usage of the term "invisible" relative to the Chinese population.

This is an expansion of the history of the Chinese from

a previous publication (Mead 2006). It is, as you will see, a tale of what would today be labeled by most as "organized terrorism" and political suppression by many including those at all levels of government. Although one should not take on guilt for such activities in the past, perhaps one can learn from them.

Chapter One

Background.

The family, as the basic unit of society, has a long history of China, although "family" as they understood it is not the same thing as people in the United States currently wish to believe in. The Confucian ethic placed the family in a primary place, stressing the need for proper conduct of relationships and holding the family system, and society in general, together with elaborate rituals. These rituals were not necessarily regimented nor arbitrary practices, but the acts of everyday life. It eventually came to mean secular ceremonial behavior and propriety or politeness that colored everyday life. Ritual in this system was understood to mean those patterns of behavior that are internalized and exert influence before actions are taken. In this manne,r people behave properly because they fear shame and want to avoid losing face. This ethical and philosophical system was developed by K'ung-fu-tzu, "Master Kong," who lived in China 551-478 B.C. It drew together the thoughts on moral, political, social, philosophical, and semi-religious concepts into a whole. In this system people were considered as being teachable, improvable, and perfectible mainly through personal and communal endeavors. Much of this was done through self-cultivation and self-creation. The stress was upon the necessity of the individual upholding the cardinal moral values.

The traditional family form was a greatly extended family consisting of the father, mother, sons, unmarried daughters, the son's wives and children, with all their relationships stretching backward in time to include family members who were deceased. It was very important for a family member to be buried with their relatives in order to maintain this multi-generational linkage.

The family was usually a very tightly-knit organization directed by the unchallenged authority of the head of the family. This person was most often the eldest male of the eldest generation still living (Lang 1968).

For the most part an individual's status within the family was recognized based upon several factors: the generation of the individual, their sex, and age, in that order (within the family), and by the families status within the larger community.

Within the Confucian system of social hierarchy, the degree holding highly educated were placed at the top. The vast farming population was given high standing and worth and were next in the system. Below them came the various groups of artisans and below them the merchants (Waley 1989).

This highly educated population occupied a position of mediation between the population at large, and the court, the ruling house. The Confucian system presupposes that an autocratic rule, exhorted to refrain from acting inhumanely toward their subjects, would understand that they would run the risk of losing the "Mandate of Heaven," the right to rule, if they do not behave correctly. Those who lost The Mandate of Heaven need not be obeyed. What this meant was that when the central government was no longer fulfilling its proper role, the general population was free of their bond to that government. The end result, after a period of unrest and frequent rebellion, would be the replacement of the old dynasty with a new one. This happened every 200-250 years or so.

The lineage tended to hold together a number of households holding the same surname. These units were most often residing within the same village but could extend outward as well.

The lineage is a patriarchal system that traces its origin backward through time to a single male ancestor.

This strict patriarchal system operated within the traditional structures within which men were held to be superior to women. This was defined by an ethical justification, by legal codes, and by long standing customary practices.

Confucianism stressed The Five Bonds: Ruler to Ruled; Father to Son; Husband to Wife; Elder Brother to Younger Brother; and, Friend to Friend. In each of these bonds, specific duties were prescribed to each of the participants. These duties also extended to the dead. In all cases, with the exception of Friend to Friend, high reverence was held for the elder. While the junior in the bonds, with the above mentioned exception of Friend to Friend, is expected to hold the elder in reverence, the senior has duties of benevolence and concern toward the junior. Social harmony results then, in part, from each individual knowing their place within the social order, and playing their part well.

Social harmony was severely disrupted during the

period just before gold was found in California. This period, known as the Opium Wars, was actually two wars, 1839-1842 and 1856-1860. Hanes and Sanello (2002) list three interlocking problems that led up to these events.

1) The Chinese belief, based upon the their very long history that stretched back for 3000-4000 years, that China represented the very pinnacle of civilization and that all others were barbarians, that is, not equals but stood in a lessor standing to the Chinese. China did not see itself as comparable to any other nation. The world as they saw it was defined as a series of successive domains with the first domain being around the imperial center and each domain surrounding the next until one reached the two outer domains: the zone of allied barbarians, and finally the zone of clueless savagery (Tuan 1974).

2) China's monopoly of tea, and to some extent luxury items such as silk and porcelain, which could only be paid for in silver bullion.

3) The emergence of Britain as a premier industrial power in the west. As a great industrial and military power, the British looked out at the world with a conviction of superiority in its Christian values, morals, ethics, and material superiority. They felt that they were, as a nation, equal, if not superior to any other, and certainly did not see themselves as members of a zone of allied barbarians or members of a zone of clueless savagery.

The end result was a cultural, political, and economic conflict with the Ch'ing Dynasty.

The Ch'ing Dynasty is usually dated as starting in 1644 when the Manchu forces seized Peking in June of that year.

By 1750, China, through a rapid economic growth, had

become the wealthiest and largest population of any of the nations of the time with a population in excess of 200 million.

By the 1790's, the imperial leadership had been, for a long time, overlooking the various levels of government corruption and inefficiency. A swell of anti-dynastic sentiment rose higher and higher, based on the feeling that the dynasty had lost The Mandate of Heaven, leading up to the White Lotus Rebellion in the 1790's (Hook 1982).

The basis of the Opium Wars stems from simple economics. By 1785 Britain was importing fifteen million pounds of tea from China, with the Exchequer levying an 100% tax on it, the government thus gaining a great amount of wealth to itself. Tea was a much greater seller in Britain than the calico, iron, and tin produced by Britain were in China. The imbalance of trade was draining Britain of silver, the only currency that China would accept. In the period 1710-1759, Britain paid 26 million pounds in silver and received 9 million pounds from China. An additional loss to the British was the drain on the Exchequer from the cost of numerous wars, including the war for independence of the colonies in the New World.

The mania for tea drinking in England began in 1658 with a mere 23 pounds being imported in 1866. But by the end of the seventeenth century the imports had risen to 20,000 pounds annually (Steiner 1979).

The solution to the trade imbalance, in the eyes of the British, was opium, a commodity produced in India and handled by the British East India Company under a Royal Charter of the British government.

The first attempt to sell opium into China failed due to a lack of interest on the part of the Chinese.

The Company then sold opium at auction in India to independent British and Indian merchants, who smuggled their product into China, for four times what it cost to grow and to process. The Company, in 1773, earned 39,000 pounds. By 1793, it was making 250,000 pounds.

By the first two decades of the nineteenth century the five thousand chests of opium sold per annum balanced the traded between China and Britain

In 1821 the British sold 4,628 chests; in 1825, 9,621 chests; in 1830, 18,760 chests; and, in 1832, 23,670 chests (Speer 1870).

While the British were not the first to sell opium into China, Arab merchants had been doing the same thing via the caravan routes since the Middle Ages when opium was used as a counter to diarrhea carried by dysentery, endemic in China, the British changed a trickle into a torrent that overwhelmed most aspects of Chinese culture and society.

The British Parliament abolished the East India Company's monopoly in China in 1833. With an open market, the amount of tea imported into Britain quadrupled. In 1833, 30,000 chests of opium were sold to maintain the economic balance of trade with opium forming about one-half of the total value of British imports into China (Speer 1870).

Through the weight of arms the British forced upon the Chinese government two treaties: The Treaty of Nanking (9 August 1842) and The Treaty of Tientsin (June 1858).

The Treaty of Nanking had the following provisions:

      1) indemnity to the British of $21,000,000 Mexican (for damages caused to them by their conflict with the Chinese);

      2) four ports, in addition to Canton, to be open

to foreign trade;

3) equal relations between Britain and China with British consuls in every port;

4) the abolition of the Cohong monopoly (a group of Chinese merchants who dealt with the foreign traders);

5) fixed tariffs on exports and imports;

6) the surrender of Hong Kong to Britain in perpetuity.

The Treaty of Tientsin had the following provisions:

1) Britain, Russia, France, and The United States would have the right to station legations in Peking (a closed city at that time);

2) Eleven more Chinese ports would be opened for foreign trade;

3) The right of foreign vessels, including warships, to navigate freely on the Yantze River;

4) The right of foreigners to travel to the internal regions of China for the purpose of travel, trade, or missionary activities;

5) China was to pay an indemnity to Britain and France of 2 million taels of silver respectively, and compensation to British merchants of 3 million taels of silver;

6) Official letters and other documents exchanged between China and Britain are banned from referring to British Officials and Subjects of The Crown by the character "yi" (meaning barbarian.)

And so it went, the steady poisoning and corrupting of

a nation, the wreckage of a government and of a people. The effects of this didn't end until 1949 when Mao's government ended the sale and consumption of opium (Hanes and Sonello 2002).

Chapter Two

Into The West Coast.

The Chinese were a major group that came to the Western United States with the initial intention of not staying. Unlike many of the other mass movements of groups into the United States, who were coming to establish new homes and new lives, the Chinese came to work, to save their money, and to return home. They were *sojourners*, that is, people who expected to live in a place temporarily to work, and then to return home. The bulk of the Chinese that came to the United States did just that. While not the only group who behaved in such a manner, they are the population that is the focus of this work. As sojourners, they saw little reason to change their living habits and cultural customs. This made them unique and it was their uniqueness that added to their problems while living in an alien culture.

The Chinese had been leaving their country for hundreds of years before they came to the United States (Ling 1912). They had filtered out into the islands of the Pacific and Indian Oceans. This out-movement was viewed with suspicious eyes by the central government. The Manchus (dynastic name - Ch'ing), who ruled China after 1644, tried to discourage this activity, by passing a ban.

When officials, whether soldiers or civil servants, illegally go out to sea, to trade or to settle on islands to live and farm, they shall be considered as conniving with rebels, and if caught, shall receive the death penalty. Magistrates found conniving in such an offense on the part of others likewise shall receive the death penalty.

Laws and Precedents of the Ch'ing Dynasty. Volume 20.

This ban was lifted locally in the province of Guangdong (Kwangtung) in 1859. In 1868, the Chinese Imperial Government reversed its order for the nation at large by signing, with the United States, the Burlingame Treaty.

The Burlingame Treaty (also known as the Burlingame-Seward Treaty of 1868), was named after the first American Minister, Anson Burlingame, to reside in Peking. He arrived in China in 1862, amended the Treaty of Tientsin and established formal friendly relations between China and the United States, ratified in Washington, D.C. in 1868 and in Peking in 1869 (Tsai 1970). The treaty contained the following provisions:

1) Recognized China's right of eminent domain over all of its territory;

2) Gave China the right to appoint consuls at ports in the United States ("to enjoy the same privileges and immunities as those enjoyed by the consuls of Great Britain and Russia");

3) Provided that "citizens of the United States in China of every religious persuasion and Chinese subjects in the United States shall enjoy

entire liberty of conscience and shall be exempt from all disability or persecution on account of their religious faith or worship in either country);

4) Granted certain privileges to citizens of either country residing in the other, the privilege of naturalization being specifically withheld.

Burlingame liked the Chinese and sympathized with their government and aided it in its problems. The Burlingame Treaty gave China "most-favored nation" privileges for visit, travel, residence, and immigration. A repeal attempt for this clause was vetoed by President Hayes (Wynn 1964). The treaty appears to have been promoted as a means of gaining large quantities of Chinese labor for building the railroads. Prior to 1865 not a single Chinese had been so employed (Hoexter 1976).

Chinese immigration to the United States was encouraged.

Chinese came from the two coastal provinces, Guangdong and Fukien. Emigrants from here made up almost the total of all emigrants from China until after the turn of the last century (1900). They started arriving in the gold fields of California in 1848, the gold fields of Australia in 1851, and were requested into the gold fields of New Zealand in 1865. They worked the sugar plantations in Hawaii by 1850. The Chinese population of Singapore rose from 54,000 to 224,000 over the time span 1866-1911; in the Dutch East Indies, 175,000 to 295,000 over the same period of years (Richie 1980; Gernet 1982).

For the United States, from the 1840's until past the

turn of the last century, the center of immigrants from China were a number of districts located in and around Guangdong (Kwangtung) Province, an area of about 80,000 square miles, slightly smaller than Oregon, which contains the ports of Guangzhou (Canton), Macao, and Hong Kong. The bulk of these districts cluster around Guangzhou. They were Sam Yap (Sam Yup, San Yup) District (comprised of Nanhai, Panyu, Shunde); the Sez Yap (Ssu Vi) District (comprised of Xinhu, Taishan, Kaiping, Enping); Huanxiang (Heung Yup, Heungshan - renamed Chungshau in 1925 in honor of its native son, Dr. Sun Yatsen) District; Sanshui District; Sihui District; Qingyan District; Zhongshan District; Zhongzin District; Boluo District; Dongguan District; Bao-an District; Huaji District; Guangding District; Gaohe District; Yangchun District; Yanhjiang District; Guanghai District; Meixinag District; and, Jieyang District. Up until World War I, sixty percent of all the Chinese in the United States came from one district included with Sze Yap, Taishan (also called Sinning, or Hsin-ning prior to 1914) while thirty percent came from Huanxiang District which contains the port of Macao. The bulk of the Chinese going to Hawaii came from Huanxiang (which is adjacent to the Sze Yap area) (Chen, J. 1980; Ow, Lai, and Choy 1973; Ohai 1980; Hsu 1971; Uchida 1960; Tsai 1970).

The people from Guangdong Province have been characterized as being enterprising, carefree, spendthrift, pugnacious, adventurous, progressive, and quick-tempered as well as being notorious for their turbulence. Within China, as a people, their bellicosity earned them a name for barbarism (an unkind remark among the Chinese). They were known for the frequency and intensity with which local groups took up arms against each other. In the 1850's and 1860's there was a period of large-scale warfare between the Hakka and the Punti (Cantonese) speakers. This on-going clash was carried into the United States (Uchida 1960). In Guangdong, as well as in Fujian, the clan members had a very strong self-identification with their respective clans and were eager to defend their clan interests against outsiders. In the numerous conflicts between the clans, over such things as water distribution, local administration, etc., the clan leadership could count upon the loyalty of the clan members. In California these disputes also surfaced in various locales. Much of this tight clan affiliation may be attributed to the fact that in the provinces of Guangdong and Fujian, the more or less compact villages (the basic rural unit in most of China) and the lineage tended to coincide. This made villages of a single lineage, a happenstance which was not usually the case elsewhere in China. This tendency of unilineal village would frequently be true for several villages situated near each other within a single district. Thus, all members of several villages would share a single family name. As an aside, it can be noted that only in Guangdong and Fujian Provinces can one find, in the villages, houses built in the modern non-Chinese style of the time which seems to indicate successful members returning to China with sufficient wealth to construct new houses architecturally based upon house styles that had been seen while abroad (Yutang 1939; Freedman 1958; Hayes 1980; Lang 1968).

This strong affiliation of clan membership and clan/district identity became very important in the United States with the development of the Chinese Six Companies in San Francisco in the early 1850's.

The movement of the Chinese leaving their country was created by conditions that pulled from the outside and pushed from the inside of China. The pulling factors were the lure of the gold fields and the shortage of laborers in the swelling industrializing processes, such as the building of the great railroad systems. The pushing factors included a dysfunctional national government which led to civil wars and the ensuing poverty and rural unemployment, natural disasters which led to famine, and to foreign intrusions and interference which helped bring about the decay of the governmental structure (Chen, C. 1972; Friday 1982 ; Hsieh 1973; Hibbert 1970; Griffin 1938; Cheng 1956; Jones 1979).

Disfunctioning Government
By the last few years of the 18th century, the national government's treasury was almost exhausted from the costs of distant wars, suppressing local revolts, and the emperor's largess. In the early 1720's-1730's, the state's reserves had amounted to about sixty million liang. But by the eve of the Tai P'ing Rebellion (1850-1864), the reserves had fallen to around nine million. As China entered the 19th century, the political and administrative system, the techniques of production, and the commercial practices were no longer adequate for an empire which now controlled a vast territory and had a population whose numbers had almost doubled in the previous hundred years. Dissatisfaction with the central government was expressed by localized rebellions. Peasant revolts inspired by the White Lotus Sect (*Pai-lien Chiao*) were not finally suppressed until 1803. But, from 1811 onward, new troubles broke out in the lower Yellow River Valley in the Provinces of Henan (Honan), Hebei (Hopei, Hopeh), and

Shandong (Shantung). These insurgents belonged to the Society of the Celestial Order (*T'ien-li-chiao*), a newer version of the White Lotus Sect.

This outbreak was finally crushed in 1814. The peasant revolts were caused by a number of factors including: land shortages; an increase in fiscal burden, i.e, taxes of every sort; the depreciation of copper (the currency utilized at the local level) in relation to silver; land ownership concentrated in the hands of a few rich landowners (especially true in the south); the fall of rent which was tied to the rapid rise in the price of land; and, small farmers being transformed into agricultural laborers.

Revolt broke out between the Provinces of Hunan and Guangxi (Kwangsi) in a mountainous area along their mutual borders, another sign of the disrepute with which the central government was held. In South China, during the first half of the 19th century, another secret society took root, one that would have long-term consequences for other areas, notably Hong Kong and the United States, the Society of the Triad (*San-ho-hui*) which was also known as the Society of Heaven and Earth (*T'ien-ti-hui*). The secret societies spun off other affiliated, equally clandestine organizations, most of them having revolutionary tendencies with religious overtones. These numerous secret societies laid the groundwork for such rebellions as the Tai P'ing, which overran much of southern China and would have probably toppled the central government except for the intervention of foreign governments who sent troops and military aid (and extracted concessions for this aid from the central government). The combination of a decaying central government and chaos coupled with sweeping poverty led to six major rebellions breaking out between 1850-1878:

The Tai P'ing t'ien-kuo (1850-1864)
The Nien (1853-1868)
The Miao of Kweichow (1854-1872)
The Hui of Yunnan (1855-1873)
The Hui of Shensi-Kansu (1863-1873)
The Hui of Sinkiang (1862-1878).

An American missionary in China at that time, Charles Taylor, wrote in his journal, July, 1853, that "The whole empire is in a ferment of excitement. Disaffection to the existing government is spreading rapidly, and signs of it are manifest in the open resistance to the oppressive demands of the Mandarins in every direction . . . "

And as it always seems to be the case, the actions of government officials did not help settle things down.

The newly appointed Viceroy Yeh Ming Shen's estates in central China were devastated by the Tai P'ing Rebellion. From June to August, 1855, he vented his anger on the people of Guangdong Province by having 75,000 people decapitated, more than half of whom had nothing to do with the rebellion. The Tai P'ing Rebellion, before it was ended, having lasted for fourteen years, had devastated 16 provinces and 600 cities with overall casualties (including both sides) of 20-30 million killed (Chen, J. 1980; Chen, C. 1972; Lyman 1970).

During this same period of time a political cleavage developed over the question of what to do about all that foreign intervention and interference that was occurring in Chinese affairs. The cleavage roughly corresponded with older political divisions between the North of China and the

South of China. The Northerners were people with little contact with foreigners while the Southerners tended to be more open minded and better informed on matters foreign. And it was from the South that the bulk of the Chinese migrated.

Natural Disasters

China was a culture heavily dependent upon an agricultural system that was in turn heavily dependent upon extensive irrigation systems and the control of water. Any major disruption to the water supply was also a major disruption to an large portion of the food supply. Between 1841 and 1843, the *Huang Ho* (Yellow River) broke through its dikes three times, inundating tens of thousands of acres and killing millions of people. In 1855, the lower *Huang Ho* burst through its banks and changed its course starting just west of the town of K'ai-feng. The river migrated from the Huai area in a northward direction into the Hsinan area, emptying into the Bo Hai (Gulf of Pohai). This new river mouth was approximately 300 miles from where the old mouth had been.

It was the worse flooding in the region in hundreds of years. Between the flooding, the destruction of property, and the loss of the water itself, vast sections of agricultural land were lost to production or made unproductive. In 1876-1879, a drought hit Shaanxi (Shensi), Shanxi (Shansi), Hebei (Hopei, Hopeh), Henan, and part of Shandong (Shantung) Provinces. With the central government totally incapable of moving supplies from one section of the country to another (a major function of the central government), 9-13 million people died. In 1847-1848, the Canton delta at the estuary of the Delta River (which is itself a combination of the alluvial sediments of the Hsi Chiang (West River), the Pei Chang (North River), and the Tung Chiang (East River), plus a network of tributaries, flooded, destroying many of the farms and enhancing the crowding in the cities (Hibbert 1970; Friday 1982; Hsieh 1973).

Poverty

The economy was crumbling. The provinces of South China, which were more sensitive to variations in the level of economic activity, probably felt the recession of the first half of the 19th century much more sharply than the North Provinces. Vast quantities of silver were lost to the British as payment for the enforced importation (by the British) of opium. This, coupled with the diversion of trade from Guangzhou (Canton) to Shanghai after the Treaty of Nanking (1842), accelerated the decline in the local economies which, in turn, impacted upon the populations of Guangdong, Guangxi, and Hunan Provinces. Between 1848-1858 the exports of tea (one of the few products sought from China by the outside world) from Guangzhou fell from 76 to 24 million pounds while exports from Shanghai rose from 3.8 to 51.3 million pounds. With the loss of the export trade, the economic recession deepened in the region around Guangzhou. By the 1870's over sixty percent of China's trade was handled through Shanghai (Jones 1979; Griffin 1938; Cheng 1956).

An entire population of boatmen, carriers, and merchants who had made their living from commercial activities, in and around the Guangzhou area, as well as along the major roads that traversed the interior valleys of Hsinag and the Kan, were ruined. These people then became ripe for the promises of the secret societies and for rebellion against the central government. It was this population which furnished the first members of the Tai P'ing rebellion. As the recession deepened a network for the exportation of labor began to develop from about 1845. Laborers were organized for shipment to the silver mines in Peru and the sugar-cane fields of Cuba. They left from the ports of Hsia-men (later called Amoy, now Xiamen), Fujian Province, and Shan-tou (Swatou) in northeastern Guangdong Province.

Foreign Intrusions and Interference

In 1773, the East India Company gained possession of the opium smuggling monopoly running from India into China. By 1810 they were moving into Guangzhou 4-5,000 cases of opium (each case weighing 133 pounds). The Chinese government issued a decree forbidding the sale of opium in 1729 and issued a series of vetoes forbidding the importation of the drug in the years 1796, 1813, 1814, 1839, and 1859.

The British trading companies, in their zeal to earn vast profits, ignored the vetoes and continued to send opium into China, a historical activity having clear resonance with the problems in the United States today.

The British companies received the full cooperation and military support of their government as well as the help of local Chinese who were also realizing large profits in aiding and abetting the drug trade.

It wasn't until 1816 that the East India Company decided to develop the opium trade systematically. The ensuing smuggling undermined the Chinese economy. Between 1820-1825 the balance of trade became heavily favored against China, and never shifted back. From

1800-1820 10 million liang of silver entered China but during this same period 10 million liang left. The out flow of silver was mainly caused by the opium trade. It continued throughout the 19th Century. From 1825 to 1835, the number of chests of opium moving into China rose from 19,000 to 35,000. By the turn of the century (1900), opium was still thirty percent of all materials imported into China. Even during the Tai P'ing rebellion 30 million liang of silver left through the port of Guangzhou alone.

In desperation, the Chinese government seized 20,000 cases of opium in Guangzhou and ordered the British Army to leave. In response, the British naval forces came up river and shelled the place with naval guns, occupied the towns of Hsia-men (Amoy), Ning-po, Tinh-hai, and threatened Hangchow and the lower Yangtse Valley. After a series of military defeats (for the Chinese troops), the so-called Opium War, the Chinese agreed to the Treaty of Nanking in 1842. In this treaty they ceded to Great Britain the port of Hong Kong and agreed to open trade, mainly the importation of opium, through the ports of Xiamen (Amoy), Shanghai, Ning-po, and Guangzhou (Canton). The British Government proclaimed Hong Kong a free port in 1842. No duties were collected and foreigners might own and employ any kind of ship. The tensions between the Chinese government and foreign governments continued with new fighting breaking out. The British in 1856, and the British and French in 1857, bombarded Guangzhou, with the British landing 5,000 troops to lay siege to the town. The Chinese government was forced to sign, in 1858, the Treaty of Tientsin, making even more concessions to the foreign governments occupying Chinese land (Griffin 1938; Cheng 1956; Beeching 1975).

Summary

From all of the above it can be seen that China during the 19th century was beset by a number of internal disasters, some of which were enhanced by external forces: failing government; failing economy; vast quantities of land lost to food production due to natural disasters; vast regions of the land in total chaos due to rebellion and warfare. The wonder of it all is not that large numbers of Chinese chose to go overseas but that so many intended to return.

Chapter Three

California

The ship *Brooklyn* left New York on February 4, 1846, headed to the west coast with members of the Church of Latter-Day Saints aboard. They had been told to flee Babylon as others had left Navoo, Illinois, following cultural clashes over such things as polygamy, land ownership, and political control.

In May, 1846, the United States declared war on Mexico. Commodore Sloat was sent to establish American authority in California.

In July of the same year, John Fremont spiked 10 Spanish guns in the Presidio and labeled the entrance to the bay "Chrysoplylae" or "Golden Gate." The population of Yerba Buena, later named San Francisco, was noted as being 1,000 non-natives with around 50 buildings. The town was essentially an island having a great ocean to the west and vast open space stretching to the east.

California was under the control of about 9,000 Californios who had tired of Mexican control and seized the territory of Alta California which then came under U.S. control by January 1847. It was, along with other territory, ceded to U.S. by the Treaty of Guadalupe Hildalgo, 2

February, 1848 which had a provision that those Mexican citizens who within a year did not elect to retain their allegiance to Mexico would automatically acquire "the title and rights of citizens of the United States" (Heizer and Almquist 1971).

The *Brooklyn* arrived in port on July 31 with 230 Mormons under the leadership of Samuel Brannan. They expected to meet the other Mormons who were crossing the country from Illinois.

In 1847, Brannan established the first newspaper, *The California Star*. That same year Yerba Buena was officially renamed as San Francisco. At this time the town had around 79 buildings which was made up of 22 shanties, 31 frame houses, and 26 adobe dwellings.

The *Californian* newspaper gives the following population figures: white 375, Indians 34, Sandwich Islanders 40, Negroes 40, a total of 459 (Williams 1930). These are interesting figures as Fremont stated over twice as many inhabitants for the year before.

In August of this year, Capt. Sutter and John Marshall entered into an agreement to build a lumber mill on the banks of the South Fork American River at a place called by the indigenous population "Culloomah," called Coloma by the settlers. The mill was constructed in 1847. The crew included a number of laborers from the disbanded Mormon Battalion, including Mr. Bennett (Sutter 1857). Gold was discovered there on January, 1848.

Anon (1848) reported that:

"Every seaport as far south as San Diego, and every interior town, and nearly every rancho from the base of the mountains in which gold has been found, to the Mission of San Luis, south, has become suddenly drained of human beings. Americans, Californians, Indians and Sandwich Islanders, men, women and children."

On February 2, 1848, an American ship, the Brig *Eagle* brought the first Chinese to San Francisco, a passage of 46 days from Canton. Currier (1928) citing Bancroft, states that the ship was a Clipper Barque. On board were an American missionary returning from China, Mr. Charles V. Gillespie, and two Chinese men and one woman. The Chinese had been brought to the United States by Gillespie to work in his home. But, shortly after their arrival in San Francisco, the two men left for the newly discovered gold fields, gold having been discovered the month before just northeast of Sacramento. The woman remained a servant in the Gillespie household (Barth 1964; Chen, J. 1980; Paul 1938/1970; Heizer and Almquist 1971; Chu 1949; Williams 1930).

Gold seekers flowed into the state from Latin America, Europe, Australia, China, and a number of states in the U.S. Nearly seven hundred ships in 1849 headed from the Atlantic ports of the United States for California (Griffin 1938).

In March, the *California Star* reported that the non-native population of San Francisco was 575 males, 177 females and 60 children. By May, the newspaper reported that whole towns were being emptied as the inhabitants rushed to the gold sites. A few days later the newspaper ceased publication as its staff joined in the rush. By October it was so bad that the U.S. Navy was offering rewards for sailors who had deserted to go to the gold fields.

In November, 1848, the U.S.S. Lexington departed San Francisco with $500,000 in gold for the U.S. mint in the East. *The California Star* and the *Californian* newspapers were combined as the *Star and Californian*. It was subsequently renamed the next year as the *Alta California* and became the first daily newspaper in California.

There were 200 deserted ships sitting in the harbor by the middle of year, 1849. But more kept coming. By November, 697 ships had arrived, 401 were American and 296 were foreign.

The British ship *Amazon* disembarked over 100 Chinese passengers in October 1849 (LaLande 1981).

In December it was estimated that the population was around 100,000 including 35,000 people who came by sea, 3,000 sailors who had deserted their ships, and 42,000 who had come overland. This was an explosive growth for just one year. The Census Bureau reported the population in San Francisco on July 1, 1850 as being 94,766.

The San Francisco Chronicle, 21 July 1878, stated that a Cantonese merchant, Chum Ming, had arrived in San Francisco and was responsible for sending the news of the gold discovery back to China. However the news made it to China, the *San Francisco Star*, 1 April 1848, noted that "two to three 'Celestials' . . . who found ready employment . . . " seems to indicate that there was a Chinese presence in the gold rush from early on (Dicker 1979). These might have been the two men brought to San Francisco by Gillespie.

Up until the gold rush, the industries of California were basically rural and simple. After 1849 everything changed. With the news of the gold rush spreading rapidly across the United States, nearly seven hundred ships left various of the Atlantic seaports and headed for San Francisco. By December 1849 California sought statehood (Lyman 1970). The Oregon constitution in its essential features reappeared in the California constitution. By 1850 the port of San Francisco was second to the port of New York for the number of ships entering and leaving. Gold hungry sailors abandoned so many ships that the lack of maritime labor effected every port around the Pacific rim. Official United States government correspondence is full of references to the excitement created in the Orient by the news of the gold rush in California (Griffen 1938; Lyman 1903).

The Chinese at home received letters from those few in California and soon the villages around Guangzhou christened San Francisco, in Cantonese, *Gum Shan*, "the Golden Mountain," or *Gum Shan Ta Fot*, "the Big City of the Golden Mountain;" in Mandarin, *Chiu Jin Shan*, "Old Gold Mountain."

Shipping companies, as well as free-lance captains, entered Chinese ports advertizing the gold discovery, offering cheap passage to California (Knoll 1982). By 1866, the Pacific Mail Steamship Company had entered the China trade having received a government subsidy of $500,000, and soon had a competitor, the Occidental and Oriental Steamship Company. Charles Crocker, an official the O.O.S.C., claimed that both lines would not have been able to make a profit if it hadn't been for the Chinese traffic. The two companies shared their facilities and docks. They made around twenty-four round trips between San Francisco and China annually (Chen 1972; Lyman 1970; Tsai 1970; McCunn 1979; Zhu 1997).

In the United States the Chinese population expanded rapidly. In 1848, an estimated 54 were in California. In 1851,

2,716 entered. In 1852, 20,026. In 1853, 16,084. In 1855, 3,324 (Chen, J. 1980; Chu and Chu 1967; Wynn 1964; LaLande 1981).

These numbers differ widely from the numbers listed by Chu (1949) in his table (Table I) of immigration figures compiled by the Reports of the Immigrant Commission. From his data there were only 40 Chinese in the state by 1848. In 1851 there were zero listed as well as in 1852. 42 Chinese entered in 1853, 13,100 in 1854, 3,526 in 1855. The numbers wavered between 2,385 - 7,518 for the years 1855-1868.

As Chu (1949) pointed out in looking at the several other sources of Chinese immigration numbers into California for the same years, the numbers vary greatly, and are often estimates rather than hard numbers. So, depending upon which citations one wishes to use, one can get a different number. Tsai (1970) lists figures from The Immigration Commission, The Bureau of Immigration, and The San Francisco Customs House (Table I) to illustrate the variation in the reported numbers of Chinese entering the country. So few Chinese women came that it wasn't until the middle of the twentieth century that there was a near balancing of the sex ratio (Lyman 1970).

The typical immigrant, or *Gum Shan Hok*, "Guest of the Gold Mountain," was a married man, usually on the young side, who had left his wife behind in the care of his parents. He hoped to make his fortune, return home, payoff the family debts, acquire land, endow the clan temple, and build a home for his parents. Very few Chinese women came to the United States. Chinese custom forbid women from leaving their homes and very few of the men came expecting to remain permanently. The best wage they could expect to earn in Guangzhou, at that time, was the equivalent of 10 cents a day.

In the United States they could earn between 50 to 75 cents a day for most forms of manual labor. The average annual remittance to China was about 30 dollars. The typical immigrant usually paid his way by borrowing on family security, or by being supported by a family member already in the United States. Many had their way paid with advance money loaned by a potential employer or labor contractor, a form of assisted passage known as the Credit-ticket system. Sometimes the money was loaned by one of the earlier arrivals, *Chiu-k'e*, "Old Sojourners," to those who wished to come, the *Hsin-k'e*, "New Sojourners," who were obligated to pay back the debt once they started to work in California. The cost of passage from China to San Francisco was usually $30-40, at that time about one year's wages (Ohai 1980; Friday 1982; Griffin 1938; Sandmeyer 1973; LaLande 1981).

The average crossing from China to San Francisco took 62 days under conditions which were frequently brutal. As an example; the *Libertad*, after a rather rapid trip (50 days) arrived in San Francisco, 19 July 1854, with 100 of her original 500 Chinese passengers dead of scurvy, a 20% mortality rate (Knoll 1982). The Chinese were most often crowded below deck, ill-fed, and frequently harshly treated. At times, the Chinese rioted and killed both captain and crew (Ow, Lai and Choy 1973: Dicker 1979). In April 13, 1850, the California legislature passed the Foreign Miners Tax that required non-American born miners to pay a monthly fee of $20 tax. This was the first anti-Chinese legislation passed in California. It was repealed on March 14, 1851. California had become the 31st state in the Union on September 9, 1850.

During the time period 1851-1854, the Chinese established in San Francisco what became known as "The Six

Companies." These were grouped around, in the main, kinship/clan lines. In China there were four types of group organizations/associations/guilds other than the clan and the family. These were craft, merchant, community, and provincial. The last of these were what the "companies" were based upon (Hsu 1971; Sandmeyer 1973). These organizations, in San Francisco, were considered *Hui kuan* (*Wui kun*) , "society" or "club" (Chu 1949). They were created and organized as follows:

1851   *Sam Yap Hui Kuan*, "The Three Districts Company," comprised of Nahai, Panyu, and the Sunde Districts (representing Guangzhou);

Sze Yap Hui Kuan, "The Four Districts Company," comprised of Xinhu, Taishan, Kaipung, and Enping Districts;

1852   *Yeong Wo Hui Kuan*, comprised of the Zhongshan (Chungshan) District;

Yan Wo Hui Kuan, (formerly named *Hip Kat Hui Kuan*) , comprised of the Hakka families of Bow On, Chak Kai, Tiung Gwoon, and Chu Mui;

1853/1854   *Ning Youn Hui Kuan*, (*Ning Yeong Hui Kuan*) Taishan who pulled out of *Sze Yap Hui Kuan* (Hoy 1942).

The *Sze Yap* were located southwest of Guangzhou. These were impoverished rural districts. Most who came from these districts were poor peasants who became laborers, domestic servants, and, in a few cases, labor contractors who negotiated work for their countrymen. Seven of out ten migrants derived their origin from this region.

The *Sam Yap* were north and adjacent to Guangzhou. The early arrivals were small merchants and skilled craftsmen.

The *Zongshan* were peasants who came from the heartland of the Pearl River Delta to the south of Guangzhou. They were the second largest group of migrants and dominated the fish markets, ladies garment factories, and the chrysanthemum and aster farms along the California coast.

Control of the companies tended to be in the hands of the merchant members. A membership fee of ten dollars was charged to all who joined (Nee and Nee 1972; Sandmeyer 1973).

The Six Companies had agents who operated out of Sacramento and Stockton, the main gateways into the gold fields. The newly arrived Chinese usually became members of one of the sections within the Six Companies. The Companies secured for their members the necessary equipment if they were going to the gold fields. The Chinese who landed in San Francisco usually remained for just a few days and then proceeded by steamer to Sacramento, Stockton, Marysville, and other ports along the San Joaquin and Sacramento Rivers. From these towns, the agents directed immigrants into the gold fields as well as acting as labor contractors or sub-contractors. As new fields opened, the Chinese appeared: Rogue River, Oregon - 1853; Pikes Peak, Colorado - 1858; the Comstock Lode, Nevada - 1859; the Boise Basin, Idaho - 1859/1860; Montana -

1864 (Ow, Lai and Choy 1973; Hoy 1942; Barth 1964; Hoexter 1976; Williams 1930; Lyman 1970).

By 1868, the Six Companies claimed to have a membership that totaled 58,3000, which, if true, must have represented the bulk of all the Chinese in the United States at that time (DeFault 1959). In 1876, it was reported in the diary of Li Kuei, who passed through San Francisco on his way to the Centennial Exhibition in Philadelphia, that about 160,000 Chinese resided in the U.S. with about 40,000 in San Francisco, the rest scattered around the other states. Li lists a total membership in the Six Companies in 1876 as between 149-168 thousand (Chu 1949).

In 1890, the Shew Hing Association joined the Six Companies with the overall name remaining unchanged (Uchida 1960).

If Chinese wanting to come to California were too poor to pay for their passage, The Six Companies paid for that passage as well as for their stay in San Francisco before they left for the gold fields. San Francisco was well-equipped by way of everything that any miner would require. The prices here were from one to three or four times less than what one would pay for the same item in the inland towns and mining regions. There was no form of contact labor, no form of economic slavery, but there was the expectation that all debts would be paid before returning to China (Williams 1930).

The Six Companies controlled all the activities within Chinatown, having a virtual monopoly. They met new arrivals at the dock, provided employment, gave them lodging and board (if necessary, until employment was found), provided medical attention, helped the infirm return to China, and arbitrated certain disputes within district associations. In addition, they provided outfitting services, postal service with Guangdung Province, medical insurance, and provided aid in the returning of the remains of the dead to their home villages. Every individual departing for home was checked at the pier to see that all his debts had been paid off. An exit tax was collected. This was a fee collected to help those who remained in the United States. The Six Companies imported foodstuffs and utensils from China and saw to their distribution inside the United States. They worked with, and sometimes duped, the Customs and Immigration officials (Nee and Nee 1972; LaLande 1981; Sandmeyer 1973; Hoyt 1974; Hoy 1942; Lyman 1970).

Before the establishment of the Chinese legation in Washington in 1878, the Six Companies functioned as the diplomatic representatives of the Chinese population, and continued to have great influence even afterwards (Tsai 1970).

The Six Companies were often used to justify the political goals of those politicians who would claim whatever advanced their agenda. A good example was M.C. George of the Oregon House of Representatives who stated on 22 March 1883 in the Oregon House (as quoted in Trull 1946) :

> ". . . It is neither the pluck or the energy, nor the brain of the individual Chinese flooding our shores, which causes them to come to America as our immigrants come from Europe. It is rather the energy of a company, an organization, a concentrtaion of corporate wealth which buys and owns, imports and sells the time and labor of those lower classes of Chinese. The Six Companys today carry on the importation of men as others do a cargo of tea. These Companies trading and trafficking in this species

of cheap labor, buy it and bring it here to compete with our American citizen laborers."

In addition to the district associations, the secret societies were also imported. The original branch of The Triad Society in California was an offshoot of the Guangdong association called, in San Francisco, *Hung Shun Tong*, "The Hall of Obedience to Hung." It was also known as *Chee Kung Tong*. Various tongs (associations or societies) developed and gradually expanded into illegal operations, each specializing in some area. The *Hip Sing Tong* controlled the gambling clubs; the *Wa Ting Shan Tong* collected tribute from the brothels; the *On Leong Tong* dealt in slave girls. The tongs greatest period of power ran from the 1880's to the 1920's (Barth 1964; Nee and Nee 1972; Dicker 1979).

In 1849, San Francisco housing was mainly tents and shanties, but, by 1853, brick construction came into favor due to the ever present fire danger to wooden structures. San Francisco had already had a series of large fires that consumed many blocks of wooden structures. A hundred acres of bayside shoreline was being filled in to make more flat land for construction while the hilly portions of town were covered with warehouses, stores and shops, hotels, business and professional offices, banks, saloons, brothels, theaters, an occasional church or school (Paul 1982). Today, much of San Francisco is built on the man-made land constructed over the original marshland, swamps, lagoons, and rocky hills that were reclaimed by Chinese laborers (Sung 1967).

Food imports began coming into San Francisco from Hongkong consigned to Chinese firms. Invoices for the years 1850-1854 reveal that the majority of the shipments contained food or potables (tea, brandy, etc.) as well as Chinaware, wooden ware, bamboo ware, lacquer ware, iron and copper pots, chopping knives, chop sticks, ladles, tongs, and mills. The foods listed by invoice included: oranges, pumelos, dry oyster, shrimp, cuttle fish, mushrooms, dry bean curd, bamboo shoots, narrow leaved greens, yams, ginger, sugar, rice, sweetmeats, sausage, dry duck eggs, dry fruit, salt ginger, salt eggs, tea oil, dry turnips, betelnut, orange skins, kumquat, duck liver, melon seed, dried duck kidneys, minced turnips, shrimp soy, chestnut flour, bird's nests, fish fins, arrowroot, tamarind, dried persimmons, dried guts, bean sauce, lily seed, beche de mer, Salisburia seed, taro, and seaweed. Most of the food stuffs were for Chinese consumption. By 1867 China had shipped more than 18-million pounds of rice to the West Coast (Spier 1958a; Hoexter 1976; Pfaelzer 2008).

By the end of the 1860's, the Chinese formed the single largest national group of miners in California. They were concentrated in the mining counties in the northern half of California, and in San Francisco, their main port of entry. By 1880, 30% of the Chinese in California were located in San Francisco. It had been suggested that they were seeking less expensive, less dangerous occupations than mining. Of course, it could have been the natural drift from the mining camps into the urban setting as mining played out. This can be seen in the shift of occupations as listed in the census data (DeFault 1959; Paul 1970; Dicker 1979).

From 1860 until 1890 Chinese fishermen were operating ocean-going junks, running a relatively important fishery operation with on-shore headquarters from San Diego in the south to near San Simeon in the north. In Marin County, on the San Francisco side of the bay, they developed (in1852) a fishing village of about 150 fishermen with twenty-five craft, catching around 3,000 pounds of fish daily. In 1854, it was reported that they were taking sturgeon, shark, and herring, all dried and packed in barrels, boxes, and sacks (Dicker 1979). The village continued to expand so that by 1873 it had thirty-two houses with a catch of 20-30 tons of shrimp each week. Chinese fishermen built three types of vessels: junks, sampans, and dinghies, constructed for the most part from redwood and modeled after what they knew from China. Junks, 30-60 feet in length, had high decks, deep keels with anchored centerboards for stability, massive rudders, and from one to three masts (Spier 1958a; Ma 1991).

The California legislature passed a tax of $4 on only the Chinese fishermen. Then they passed legislation prohibiting the types of nets they used and in the 1880s another tax on their fishing, essentially eliminating all Chinese fishing activities in the state (Steiner 1979).

As people spread out from Sutter's Mill seeking gold further and further north and south, so did the Chinese. Chinese mining and miners extended from the Feather River and it branches in the north to Mariposa in the south, an area that lies on the western slopes of the Sierra Nevada Mountains. While the mountains range up to 14,000 feet, the gold district itself varies in altitude from 200 to 3,000 feet, more or less, although most of the gold was found between 1,500 - 2,800 feet. The district is about 180 miles long by 25 miles wide. It stretches across the modern counties of Plumas, Sierra, Yuba, Nevada, Placer, El Dorado, Amador, Calaveras, Tuolumne, and Mariposa. All the gold bearing rivers in this area flow into either the San Joaquin or Sacramento Rivers. The classic path followed by miners led from the Bay of San

Francisco and up either the San Joaquin or Sacramento Rivers, a trip that could take up to a week and cost $16 or more. Chinese working in these mines were paid $1 - $2 a day. (Williams 1930). Only in the northern mining areas was hydraulic mining utilized. The sluicing technology developed in California was later introduced into New Zealand by miners migrating there (Ritchie 1981). Anthony Chabot, a Nevada County miner came up with the idea of directing a powerful spray of water, supplied by ditching, to work the deposits. Tinsmith Eli Miller, working with Chabot and E.E. Matteson, is said to have developed a tapered metal nozzle to create an even stronger jet of water. The early effort utilizing canvas hose gave way to riveted iron pipe and large high-pressure nozzles called "giants" (LaLande 1981, 1983).

Chinese crews were often employed to dig the ditches and construct the flumes to deliver the water to where it was required. In 1869, there were over 6,000 miles of ditching located in the southern Sierra to the Siskiyou Mountains (LaLande 1981).

The Chinese formed two types of settlements in the mining districts of California: camps, generally located on the banks of rivers and their tributaries, and Chinatowns, build inside the various towns. The camps were separate communities comprised of only Chinese miners and were generally tents and brush structures. The Chinatowns were distinct quarters within the mining towns and provided restaurants, laundries, and shops where articles of all sorts could be purchased as well as serving as supply centers for the outlying Chinese camps. In 1851 neither of these settlement types were evident as mining was by individuals primarily. By 1852, camps and Chinatowns began to come into existence. "Chinatown" sections had formed in the towns of Grass Valley, Placerville, Coloma, Shasta, Yuba, and Weaverville (Rohe 1982; Williams 1930). The Chinatowns have been suggested to have been, at least partially, a self-imposed ghetto (LaLande 1981).

Nevada City, built in the center of a rich gold district, had the largest Chinatown in the northern gold region. It was a center of Chinese distribution for supplies for the mining activity lying between the Auburn and Feather Rivers. The Auburn Chinatown was the center of Chinese activity for the North Fork of the American River and the area extending from Roseville to Colfax in the south and Dutch Flat in the north. The Chinatown in Angels Camp was the center of Chinese mining for all of southern Calaveras County. Chinese Camp, or, China Camp, the town founded by the Chinese in 1849, was the Chinese center in the entire mining region with the Chinese Six Companies having their principal offices outside of San Francisco located here. China Camp, located near Sonora, was likely the first all-Chinese town in the United States, built by Chinese that had been purged by white miners from their claims at Camp Salvado, had a population of 2,000 (Pfaelzer 2008; Rohe 1982). There were also offices of the Six Companies in Sacrament, Stockton, Folsom, and Angels Camp (DuFault 1959; Ow, Lai and Choy 1973; Williams 1930).

Upon arrival to the gold fields the Chinese were often directed to old claims, abandoned by other miners as worthless. The miners were happy to sell these claims to the Chinese as the sellers went off to what they felt were better spots. The Chinese worked these "worthless" claims and recovered the gold left behind by the coarser methods of the previous occupants (Williams 1930). It would appear that by doing this they irritated those who felt that they had played some clever trick upon the Chinese.

The *Sacramento Daily Union* (February 1859) reported that 75 per cent of the Chinese population in the state were engaged in mining. The 1860 Census reported than 24,282 Chinese out of 34,934 worked as miners (Rohe 1882).

Like all frontier communities, San Francisco suffered from a scarcity of labor enhanced by loss to the gold fields. Women were very few and the Chinese supplied the need for cooks, laundrymen, etc., as well as that of the heavier work in the mines. San Francisco, in the Census of 1850, had a female population of less than 8% (Sandmeyer 1973; Dicker 1979). There were around 700 Chinese in the city. An area labeled "little Canton," or perhaps "Little China," had 33 retail stores, 15 pharmacies, and 5 restaurants serving whoever walked in the door (Sowell 1996; Chu and Chu 1967).

For almost a generation in the early period of San Francisco the jobs usually filled by those who cook, clean, wash, and sew were lacking. Even by 1880, there were only three females for every five males of all races and only one child of school age to every three to four adults. Any woman or youth that wished to find work could. The Chinese often became gap-fillers, taking those jobs of menial, petty, and laborious work which the white men would not do. During this period the Chinese were a considerable and indispensable element in California progress (Collidge 1909).

When the Chinese entered the laundry business, the price of laundering a dozen shirts dropped from $8 to $2. The first wash-house was opened by Wah Lee on Jackson Street, San Francisco, in the Spring of 1851 (Ong 1983). Much of the drop in cost is attributed to doing the job locally. Often, before, laundry had been shipped to Canton or Honolulu to be washed and then sent back by return steamer. It frequently was cheaper to buy new clothes than have them cleaned/washed in this manner (Dicker 1979). The laundry business came into existence due to the shortage of women who traditionally provided these services. The Chinese had no problem doing "women's work" which had been inhibiting the white males from his occupation " (Lyman 1970). By 1870, in San Francisco, the Chinese dominated the laundry trade with around 2,000 in operation (Sowell 1996).

In 1860, California had a greater export trade than the state of Pennsylvania, which was a radical shift in the commercial pattern in the United States. During the 1860's, several companies specialized in carrying merchandise to and from China. The most well known of these included Macondary and Company, the Pacific Mail Steamship Company, and the Occidental and Oriental Steamship Company (Griffin 1938; Jones 1979; McCunn 1979).

Between 1850-1880 the Chinese population in the United States (being mainly in California) went from 7,520 to 105,465 (although the U.S. Census only listed 758 for 1850). In 1870 the Chinese comprised 8.8% of the total population in California, yet they represented 25% of the wage-earning force (Takaki 1979).

The first two Governors elected under the State Constitution of 1850 (Peter Burnett, John McDougal) were friendly to Chinese immigration into California (Williams 1930).

The first instance of anti-Chinese violence occurred early in either 1849 when about 600 Chinese were driven off their mines by a party of whites or 1852 when sixty miners from Mormon Bar, on the American River, attacked a Chinese camp and drove out the two hundred Chinese miners. The 1852 attackers, accompanied by a marching band, then assaulted a Chinese settlement at Horse Shoe Bar and expelled four hundred Chinese miners from there. An English nobleman, Sir Henry Huntley, traveling there at the time stated that this happens only because the Chinese will work for much less wages than the discontented white miners. Another English observer stated that the whites acted "against any placer inhabited by colored people, if it were worth appropriating or excited their cupidity." (Williams 1930; Lyman 1970; LaLande 1981; Pfaelzer 2008).

Miners in various of the mining districts passed resolutions stating that they wished to stem "this Asiatic inundation that threatens to roll over the State . . . " and "for the purpose of protecting themselves from this influx of the degraded inhabitants of China" (Williams 1930).

Many of these white miners were from the Southern states and brought with them their virulent racial attitudes (Sowell 1996).

The Chinese camp on the Yuba River was raided and over thirty thousands dollars stolen. When appealing to the authorities, the Chinese were told that "they ought to have been able to protect themselves." The Chinese were chased from Vallecito, Douglas Flat, Sacramento Bar, Coyote Flat, Sand Flat, Rock Creek, Spring Creek, and Buckeye (Williams 1930; Lyman 1970).

The California Legislature, 1852, passed the Foreign Miners License Tax of $3. In 1853 the tax rose to $4 a month. In 1855, it rose to $6. Many Chinese miners then entered other occupations which caused the counties to lose thousands of dollars in revenue. In 1856, the Legislature repealed the increase and took it down to $4 per month (Williams 1930).

Takaki (1979) cites the 1854 California Supreme Court Case, *People v. Hall*, that stated "No black or mullato person, or Indian shall be allowed to give evidence in favor of, or against a white man." And further "Held, that the words, Indian, Negro, Black, and White are generic terms, designating races. That, therefore, Chinese and all other people not white, included in the prohibition from being witnesses against whites."

In 1856, Chief Justice Murray of California declared that the Chinese were "Indian" under the statue that disallowed Indians from giving testimony in California courts. His logic was that "Asiatics" migrated to the American continent across the Bering Strait and "descended" into Indians and were thus unable to testify in court either "in favor of or against a white man" (Williams 1930; Pfaelzer 2008; Hong 1925).

Agoston Haraszthy, called the "father of California's wine industry," hired, in 1860, 100 Chinese to work in his vineyards and winery (Dicker 1979).

The Reverend A.W. Loomis in the 1869 *Overland Monthly*, wrote "On many ranches all the laborers are people whose muscles were hardened on the little farms of China . . . Go through the fields . . . the vineyards and orchards, and you will learn that most of fruits are gathered or boxed for market by this same people" (quoted by Steiner 1979).

The first transcontinental railroad, first called the Pacific Railroad, and then the Overland Route, was built between 1863 and 1869 by the two major competitors, the

Central Pacific Railroad of California (heading east) and the Union Pacific Railroad (heading west). The construction and operation of this continent girding railroad was authorized by the Pacific Railroad Acts of 1862 and 1864 during the American Civil War with Congress supporting these acts with 30-year U.S. government bonds and extensive land grants of government-owned land. The bulk of the engineers and surveyors were Army veterans who had gained their experience during the Civil War.

To fund the Central Pacific, Collis Huntington found four partners: Mark Hopkins, his business partner; James Bailey, a jeweler; Leland Stanford, a grocer, future Governor of California, and founder of Stanford University; and Charles Crocker, a dry-goods merchant and eventual owner of Crocker Banks.

They were required to build 50 miles in the first year, and 50 miles each following year, They would receive $16,000 per mile for easy grade; $32,000 per mile in the high plains; and, $48,000 per mile in the mountains, in the form of the government bonds which they could sell to raise additional funds. They were granted a right-of-way of 400 feet plus additional land adjacent to the track for every mile built. The Central Pacific laid a total of 690 miles of track.

Between 1866-69, the Central Pacific Railroad, whose labor was approximately 90% Chinese, had an estimated savings of $5.5 million by employing Chinese laborers over non-Chinese laborers. Once they were recruited by American labor contractor's agents, such as the Sisson, Wallace, and Company for whom worked Judge E.B. Crocker, the brother of Charles and former chief justice of the Supreme Court of California, and legal counsel to the Central Pacific Railroad

(Saxton 1995), or Koopmanschap & Co. (owned and operated by Cornelius Koopmanschap, born in Weesperkarspel near Amsterdam, 31 February 1828). In late July 1865 the first gangs of laborers hired in China by Koopmanschap arrived in the railroad camp. The rate at which the recruited Chinese could be put to work was totally dependent upon the availability of shipping space (Barth 1964; Hoexter 1976; Spier 1958b). Non-Chinese laborers costs to the railroad were figured as being about one-third higher due to the fact that white workers were paid wages plus board and lodging while the Chinese were expected to take care of their own board and food (Takaki 1979). The Chinese were paid between $1 to $3 dollars per day. It was a wage which was, at that time, 6.5-8.75 times the wage of farm laborers in the area from which they had emigrated. Eventually the Chinese built 15 tunnels for the Central Pacific, the longest, summit tunnel, was 1,659 feet long, by about 32 feet high and 16 feet high. The average daily progress in tunnel construction was around 0.85 - 1.18 feet. By the time the construction was over and the two railroads joined, Chinese workers of the Central Pacific numbered 9,000 out of the total 10,000 (Clyde and Beers 1966) or perhaps nine tenths of 14,000 (Sowell 1996). Crocker estimated that at one time they had from ten to twelve thousand Chinese working on the project (Chu 1949).

A contest was held between the two competing railroads on 29 April 1869 to see which outfit could lay the most track between 7 a.m. and 7 p.m. The Chinese set the world track-laying record of more than ten miles, putting down 25,800 ties, 3,520 lengths of rail, and driving 55,000 spikes (Dicker 1979).

The former Surveyor General of California estimated

in the mid 1870s that Chinese labor on reclamation projects and railroad construction was worth about $289,700,000 to the economy of California (Steiner 1979).

In 1869 the North Pacific Coast Railroad was begun, running from Sausalito in the south to the Russian River in the north. The railroad construction utilized thirteen hundred labors, which by the next year (1870) were all Chinese. It opened for business in 1875 (Ma 1991).

In addition to these railroads, the Chinese worked on the Southern Pacific, the Northern Pacific, the Virginia and Truckee in Nevada, the Eureka & Palisades, the Carson and Colorado, the California and Oregon, the Seattle and Walla Walla, the Texas Pacific, the Houston and Texas Central, the Alabama and Chattanooga, as well as numerous other smaller lines (Steiner 1979; Saxton 1995; Currier 1928).

By 1870, 26% of the total Chinese population of the state lived in San Francisco. The city was considered by Internal Revenue Service returns as the ninth leading manufacturing city in the United States. The Workingmen's Party was organized in the same year by Dennis Kearney, an Irishman by birth, who argued against capitalists in general, and the Chinese in particular (Tsai 1970).

W.H. Martin, the general agent of the California Immigrant Union, in a statement in his report of January, 1875 stated:

> Chinamen work willingly for 75 cents to $1 per day. We have a large supply, and they soon learn and perfect themselves in any department of business. They are a necessary evil at present, for the reason that most of the young men of our State, and new-comers

generally, will not work for small wages. As
soon as this is remedied by an importation of
Eastern and European labor willing to work
for $1 to $1.50 per day, the employment of
Chinese will gradually be diminished (Chu
1949).

Chinese workers were 46% of the labor force in four major industries: boot and shoe; woolens; cigar and tobacco; and, sewing. In 1880, 52% of the boot and shoe, 49% of the brick makers, 84.4% of the cigar makers, 32.7% of the woolen mill operators were Chinese; as well as 50% of the shrimp fishing industry (Takaki 1979; Sowell 1996). In the years 1876-1906, Chinese made over 50% of the crews on American ships traveling up and down the west coast and between the United States and China (McCunn 1979).

A writer in 1869 listed the economic activities of the Chinese in California as: woolen factories; knitting mills; railroad building; highway and wharf construction; borex beds; farms; dairies; hop plantations; small fruit farms; kitchens; wood cutting; land clearing; potato digging; salt works; liquor manufacturing; cigar and cigarette making; the manufacture of slippers, pantaloons, vests, shirts, drawers, overalls, shoes; tin shops; shoe blacking, fishing; gardening; poultry and pig raising; peddling; cabinet making; carving; whips and harness making; brick making; washermen; house servants; coal heavers; deck hands; cabin servants; sailors; mining; vineyard laborers; and, laborers in the tule lands (Sandmeyer 1973).

The Chinese mainly came to the United States to make money and then go home. In the time period 1848-1882, approximately 300,000 Chinese arrived in San Francisco and

151,000 departed for China. In the time period 1882-1892, 80,000 arrived while 109,000 departed (Steeves 1984, quoting Collidge 1909).

The status of the Chinese coming into North America has been the subject of much debate with arguments over whether they were free agents or something else. The term "Coolie" in Chinese means "rent muscle," while others have stated that it meant "bitter strength." The term had been used as a word of degradation in India by the British colonial officials to mean a "beast of burden" (Steiner 1979). It was applied during the nineteenth century to the Chinese who went to the Spanish Americas as virtual slaves. Applying the term to the Chinese who entered California is to misconstrue the reality of their situation (Williams 1930; Tsai 1970). Barth (1964) proposed that the Chinese were slaves of a subtle Chinese control-system of debt-bondage rather than free or independent laborers. He suggested that while some of the immigrants were hired by foreign importers or Chinese merchants as contract laborers, the majority of them were indentured: dependent upon the credit-ticket system "under which they obtained their passage from Chinese merchants who were reimbursed by relatives of the travelers or by their future employers." Thus, in Barth's view, the Chinese merchant-creditor, through an exploitation of the laborer's personal loyalty to family and clan in China, relegated the immigrant to a condition of servility (LaLande 1981).

Barth's position has been criticized for his almost exclusive use of English source material. Tsai (1970), employing numerous Chinese sources in a recent Ph.D. dissertation on Chinese exclusion, concluded: "Barth's thesis is very imaginative, but source materials . . . prove that his arguments are not soundly based and his conclusions are wrong." The majority of evidence seems to suggest that the Chinese population was comprised of free laborers and not indentured-slaves. Coolidge (1909) asserts that the Chinese "were all perfectly free immigrants, at the very worst coming on money borrowed at a high rate of interest." Tsai (1970) stated: "The Chinese who came to the United States were free and independent emigrants."

Chapter Four

Oregon

In the placer-mining areas of eastern Oregon as in other mining areas, the Chinese miners followed the white miners, providing the manual labor to build the water transportation ditches necessary for placer mining. They frequently reworked abandoned placer claims, as these were all they were allowed to buy, and rarely attempted to stake new claims or own productive ones.

Yet despite laws prohibiting some Chinese from owning or working mining claims, many were still able to obtain them. In Prairie City, ca. 1870, it was stated that:

> "tailings of the old placer claims had been either leased or sold to the Chinese . . ." (WHPC 1902a).

Claims frequently were owned by a Chinese "company." These companies comprised from ten to twenty men (Steeves 1984). Edson (1974), in his study of the Chinese populations in eastern Oregon, utilizing the original census tracts, stated:

> While the original census reports show an average grouping of about ten to fifteen Chinese per residence, only once during the period under study do such reports specifically mention Chinese companies. The

1880 Original Schedules for John Day in Grant County enumerates several Chinese mining companies and their employees. Among the companies listed were: Ah Buck Co., twenty-four men; Yung Gon Co., eighteen men; Wan Goon Co., Ah Gin Co., and Tong Goose Co., eleven men each; and Po Un Co., ten men. The Chinese played an integral, although isolated, part in this rapid development of eastern Oregon; for in 1870, the Chinese comprised 61 percent of all the miners in the region, a figure which by 1880 had risen to 73 percent.

Statements made relative to the Chinese working on building the great railroads give some insight into the wage scale the Chinese miners and mining companies would have received. Working for the railroads, the white laborer wanted $2.00 per day and board. The Chinese companies accepted $31-35.00 per month per man and provided food and all other necessities. Single Chinese laborers working in the mines received about $1.00-1.25 per day, which rose to $1.75-2.00 by 1870 (Wynn 1964; Takaki 1979 ; DeFault 1959).

The Chinese Camps

The Chinese mining camps were often purposely located a distance away from American camps in an effort to lessen the potential for hostile acts. They were almost invariably located on a flood-free terrace overlooking a major stream, but at times (especially during the early mining period prior to sophisticated hydraulic technology) they were situated right next to a river, adjacent to the placer diggings (Williams 1930; Chiu 1967).

These camps typically utilized several types of shelters including log cabins, tents, and brush huts. Woods (1851) described a wide assortment of crude dwellings built by the non-Chinese Forty-Niners in California:

> Most . . . even in winter, are tents. Some throw up logs a few feet high, filling up with clay between the logs. The tent is then stretched above, forming a roof . . . Those who have more regard to their own comfort or health, erect log or stone houses, covering them with thatch or shingles. I have seen some very good houses at Aqua Frio made and roofed with slate. Some comfortable wigwams are made from pine boughs thrown up in a conical form, and are quite dry. Many only spread a piece of canvas or a blanket, over some stakes above them, while not a few make holes in the ground, where they burrow like foxes. The covers of these sometimes extend above ground, and are roofed with plaster or clay, looking like so many tombs. The Mexicans and Chilinos [Chileans] put up rude frames, which they cover with hides. In two cases I have seen a kind of basket, looking like a large nest, made fast among the branches, high up in the trees. These may have been used by the Californians to guard against wild beasts.

A number of types of shelters were mentioned in the literature.

Cabins - The early cabins were generally log structures with canvas, sod or shake roofs. In many areas the Chinese frequently moved into vacant cabins after the white owners had left for the latest gold strike elsewhere. They also built their own log cabins, using the corner-notched walls and horizontal roof purlins construction systems favored by many of the white miners. Most accounts, in discussing Chinese dwellings, mention them as having very small dimensions and many occupants. One nineteenth century newspaper account mentions "companies of 20 or 30 Chinese inhabiting close cabins, so small that one . . . would not be of sufficient size to allow a couple of Americans to breathe in it." Many of these cabins may not have had chimneys. Whatever the roof construction, early cabins, whoever built them, often had no ceiling or only a partial loft. The use of horizontal logs to form bearing walls has been assumed by many to be not part of the Chinese architectural tradition. However, Knapp (1986) shows a type of log house found in the northwest and southwest regions of China which, except for the roof line, is very much like the standard log house seen in the United States. Later Chinese miners also erected vertical lumber shacks at their camps, sometimes made from the boards of abandoned mining flumes (Shay 1876; Walling 1884; Coolidge 1909; Barth 1964; LaLande 1981).

A-frame - The simple "A-frame" (or walled) canvas tent was a Euro-American shelter adopted by the Chinese. These were frequently employed at very short-term sites such as railroad construction camps, but were also common in the mines. The A-frame tents had floor dimensions of about five feet by eight feet, and a height of around four feet (LaLande 1981; Ow, Lai, and Choy 1973).

Cloth Tent - The small cloth tent, with a pole supporting each end, was probably very similar to the four-foot high straw-mat tents sometimes used by the poorest class of Kwangtung peasants (Conwell 1871).

Brush Hut - Another reported form of shelter was the brush hut, constructed out of whatever vegetation happened to be at hand. An Irish miner, James Galloway, quoted in Shay (1876) said that the Chinese put up "brush tents . . . with posts and poles, and brush thrown over them." Chinese miners are said to have built similar shelters, "roofed with logs and brush," along the Chelan River in central Washington (Steele 1904). A British visitor to the California mines describes the construction of one:

> . . . the Chinese carpenter and ourselves speedily felled some young saplings, and driving two strong posts in the ground, we fixed a long spar longitudinally; on this spar rested the saplings and branches in inclined position; then placing turf at the bottom, our bush-hut was finished that night (Shaw 1973).

Tent Platforms - LaLande (1981), in his study of Chinese in the mining areas of southwestern Oregon, reported campsites with excavated terrace platforms (Squaw Creek camp, upper China Gulch camp) but that these yielded little or no archaeological evidence of superstructures. He suggested that these sites may have had ephemeral shelters such as the tents or brush huts described above. In his study he found that a local store, The Kubli Store, sold "stakes" and "sail needles" to some Chinese miners, which may have been utilized in the erection and repair of canvas tents. What he found notable about these short-term occupation sites was the excavation of level, rectangular platforms into the slopes, and the buttressing of these platforms with dry-stone reinforcing walls.

Diet

As early as 1852 quantities of food and domestic utensils were being shipped from Hong Kong to the United States, via San Francisco, all consigned to Chinese firms. The varieties of food coming in indicated that the Chinese ate very much as they had done in China and, in general, had a much more well-rounded diet than their non-Chinese contemporaries.

Few records have been reported as to what the Chinese in the mining districts actually bought. However, at the Kubli Store in Jackson County, the most commonly purchased food items were: soy sauce, ginger, almspice (alum), cinamon, red peppers, chee ma (sesame seed), muck gah (molasses-like sweetener), foo chuck (soybean curd or beansteak), salt fish, "fisch" (sardines?), oysters, codfish, "scrimps" (dried shrimp), black beans, "Nuts" (probably litchee nuts), "bamboo" (probably bamboo shoots), mugoe (white mushrooms), makkets (?), "vermiselles" (noodles), Mamasilla (noodles), salt beans, hung tah (dried vegetables), dry cabbage, chim chim toy (dried vegetable flavoring), mamoo (?), chung toy (salted radish), yung toy (dried vegetable), sill toy (dried cabbage), mintsteak (?), ham and bacon, teat, flor, "salaratus" (a mid-nineteenth century rising agent made from potassium bicarbonate), cooking oils and lard, small quantities of rice and butter, salt and sugar. This store obtained Chinese import items from Tung Chung and Company, San Francisco (LaLande 1981).

It was noted in the contemporary accounts of the time that the Caucasian workers ate beef, beans, bread and potatoes eternally. It was the Chinese diet which protected them from scurvy which affected many of the whites. The

Chinese preference for tea, made from boiling water, tended to keep them from dysentery (Hoexter 1976; Dicker 1979).

Dress

In western Oregon, the Chinese were noted as wearing a skull-cap, a collar, a long blue coat, a belt, blue trousers, white stockings, and cloth shoes, generally serge for the uppers, with leather and cork (or wood) soles. They were low cut, offering no protection for the ankle. The records from the Kubli Store in southern Oregon indicate that the Chinese purchased regular leather boots, shoes, woolen socks, western-style felt hats, "checkered shirts," "flannel" overshirts, "duck" pants, coats and gloves (LaLande 1981).

Personal Grooming

The Chinese in the camps regularly took hot-water sponge baths and changed their clothes before the evening meal. In southwestern Oregon, the Kubli Store records sales of "Chinese soap" and brushes, probably hair brushes. Regular barbering has been reported from various accounts (LaLande 1981).

Northeastern Oregon

In October, 1861, gold was discovered in Griffin's Gulch. Early the next year the word had spread and a town came into existence. Auburn was organized on June 17, 1862, in what was known as the Blue Canyon Mining District (McArthur 1974; Spreen 1939). The town had been laid out on June 13 by William H. Packwood, and others. Packwood had arrived with a longtime friend, George H. Abbott, and soon thereafter, the two men along with Knight organized a merchandising, freighting, packing company, Abbott and Packwood had experience in this business from their days on the Oregon Coast. The newly formed organization set up a portable steam sawmill. This was a period of the rapid grown of Auburn as a typical mining "boom" town. By July 20, 1862, the town had grown to 50-60 houses and a population of 250-300. Auburn had three stores, two saloons, two blacksmith shops, three butcher shops, one boarding house and the sawmill set up by Packwood and company (Spreen 1939). In the fall of 1861, after 3,000 miners had left Auburn to go to the Boise gold fields, a meeting was held and it was decided to allow the Chinese to labor in the mines (Chen, C. 1972).

A number of small water ditches were constructed by small groups of men for their private use but nothing was constructed on a large scale for general usage. In September 15-20, 1862, Packwood organized the Auburn Water Company, which included Abbott, Henry Fuller, Ira Ward of Griffin's Gulch, and others. A ditch was surveyed by A.C. Goodrich, who had surveyed and supervised the construction of the Big Oak Flat ditch in California. It was the beginning of Packwood's numerous water developments, that is, ditch building to bring water to mining areas (Spreen 1939). In November the Company was sold to a group of Portland capitalists who changed the name to The Auburn Canal Company. Auburn swelled with population to 5,000-6,000 by December 1862 (Spreen 1939).

The Chinese began to move into the eastern Oregon mining districts almost as soon as they were discovered/opened. In the 1860's, a Sam Yap group left Jacksonville in southwestern Oregon headed for the John Day gold areas near Canyon City (Barlow and Richardson 1979). The usage of this clan organization name suggests a rather direct link with the Six Companies in San Francisco. Gold had been discovered in this area in 1862 and traffic immediately developed between the area and California with miners, including the Chinese, coming by land and sea. The sea route was from San Francisco to Astoria, Portland, and the Dalles. From the Dalles it was wagon traffic to John Day. For the Chinese it was usually a long walk (Chen, C. 1972). During this same time period the Chinese were noted as reworking the clay deposits discarded by the white miners in the Rock Creek District of Baker County and making $15-20 per day doing it (Edson 1974).

During the winter, miners spread from Auburn searching for new gold deposits. And they found them. Additional sites were located in the upper reaches of the Grande Ronde River, on Burnt River and Willow Creek, and on Eagle Creek and Goose Creek. Placer mining started in 1863 at the head of Maiden Gulch. Another mining center developed at Canyon City. From these two areas the miners spread out over a large area that stretched from Canyon City to the Snake River (Dicken and Dicken 1979). The site in Maiden Gulch was soon named Kooster after one of the two miners first on the site, Tom Kooster (sometimes spelled Koster). Further north, in Shanghai Gulch, placer mining was started by Squire Morris and Neales Donnelly (Baxter 1977).

But by 1868, the boom was over and Auburn was abandoned (Hudson 1978). This was noted in the June 20, 1868 issue of *The Dalles Weekly Mountaineer*: " . . . such is fate, and Auburn will soon be China Town in every sense of the word." This same message was carried by the *Bedrock Democrat* (Baker City) in which it was noted that "There is only one company of white men at work on Griffin's Gulch, but there are several Chinamen there" (Bright 1961).

On May 19 (or May 14), 1866, a band of Paiute Indians attacked a company of 40-50 Chinese near Battle Creek, Baker County (or the Boise region of southwest Idaho) with only one member of the Chinese party surviving to tell the story (Edson

1974; Wynn 1964).

During this early period of placer mining, Packwood, Rufus Perkins, and others organized the Burnt River Ditch and Mining Company. They built Clark's Creek ditch and laid out a line in the fall of 1863 to run water for the Burnt River mines. The line was surveyed in 1864 by C. Barrett, initially a distance of 88 miles (Spreen 1939). This same year, 1864, Packwood sent A. C. Goodrich over to Kooster to survey a line to bring water to the placer works there. Simultaneously with this survey, D. S. Bronk and A. Petrie laid out and cut a ditch from West Eagle Creek to the placer works at Hogem on Goose Creek (Bronk deposition, Court Case 1488).

On August 8, 1864, Elisha and Joseph C. Packwood, uncles of W. H., filed a water right:

> ... claim the right to all the water flowing in the South West Fork of Goose Creek and intend to. turn the same into a ditch for mining purposes. Commencing at an Alder Tree marked E. P. in Canyon at a point (3/4) of a mile above where the wagon road crosses and running thence along the foot hills on the N.E. side of said creek tapping and taking in the waters of all the tributaries of said west in southwest fork of Goose Creek.

The Petrie and Bronk ditch, in bringing large quantities of water from West Eagle Creek to the head of Susan Gulch and from there into Goose Creek, stimulated the building of a number of smaller ditches for mining purposes. These smaller ditches are reflected in transactions in the County Courthouse records.

14 August 1865, V. Towner sold to W. W. Ross, for $64.70:

one water ditch beginning at the crossing on the North Fork Goose Creek about 50 yards below the residence of S.T. Packwood [another uncle of W R.] and running down the left hand side or bank of said creek to the quartz mill or arastra of (V. Towner). Also one quartz mill or arastra situated on the north fork of Goose Creek (Book A, Mining Deeds, pp: 29).

14 September 1865, George Tatum sold to I.E. Roper, for $56.00:

1/6 interest of a certain water ditch in Summit Mining District. . . . known as the South Gulch Ditch commencing (and tapping the ditch of A. Petrie) at the east end of the flume at the head of Susan Gulch and running on the south side of the hill until it reaches the head of' South Gulch (Book A, Mining Deeds, pp: 309).

10 October 1865, A. J. Vicent sold to W. W. Ross, for $50.00, a ditch:

commencing at the mouth of said ditch about 200 yards (more or less) below the quartz arastra of Towner, Wilkes & Co., and running down on the south side of Goose Creek to the Neill (sp?) claims (Book A, Mining Deeds, pp: 64).

On November 7, 1865, Petrie and Bronk borrowed $3,800 from Thomas A. Pope and E. Smalley putting up their ditch as collateral. Their repayment schedule lists Augusta, Union County, as a place name. In addition the courthouse document states:

. . . located and described as follows commencing at a point by the west fork of Eagle

Creek a distance of eleven miles more or less to
the mining camp of "Hogem" in said mining
district . . .

This document suggests that Hogem is probably located
in Susan Gulch, the gulch into which Petrie and Bronk ditch
discharges. Susan Gulch was one of the gulches mentioned
frequently in the courthouse records as a place where a large
number of placer claims were being bought and sold.

15 August 1866, Isham B. Roper sold W. W. Ross, for
$20.00 all rights in [the South Gulch Ditch] (Book A, Mining
Deeds, pp: 309).

27 August 1866, John F. Perider sold to W. W. Ross, for
$10.00, 1/6 interest in the South Gulch Ditch (Book A, Mining
Deed, pp: 311).

8 December 1866, V. Turner sold to W. W. Ross for
$75.00:

a certain water ditch about twelve miles in length
running from Eagle Creek in Union county to a
mining camp known as Augusta and Hogem, said
ditch being known as the Petrie and Bronk water
ditch (Book A, Mining Deeds, pp:305).

The year after forming and selling the company to build
the El Dorado ditch, W. H. Packwood decided to build a ditch
to supply water to the Kooster area and sent Rufus Perkins to
make a survey.

After hearing Perkin's report on the Kooster area and
upon what he saw vis a vis the water supply, Packwood took
C. M. Foster, the civil engineer, Alex Stewart, a man called
Williams (W.C.?) and Charle Awah, Packwood's Chinese
interpreter and scribe and then administrator on the later
Sparta Ditch project, and ran a preliminary line for a water

ditch to supply the mines (Steeves 1984; Rand 1974). The group probably started in or about mid-October as Foster stated in his court deposition (Court Case 1488) that he talked with Fisk in October about the Petrie and Bronk ditch. They worked until deep snow stopped them, returning to Auburn in November. Packwood changed Goodrich's line, surveyed in 1864, by planning drops rather than a continuous grade in order to successfully negotiate the terrain from his water source to Kooster and vicinity. Shortly after returning from the field, Packwood arranged with J. W. Virtue, a banker in Baker City, to draw $10,000 in cash. I. B. Bowen and Ed Carnston donated $16,000 in supplies and merchandise. The Eagle Canal Company was founded, Rufus Perkins, Ed Cranston, and I. B. Bowen each donating $10,000 to the operation, each receiving a 1/5 interest. The officers were:

R. Perkins - President

E. P. Cranston - Treasurer

W. H. Packwood - Secretary and Engineer. Charley Awah (at times in the contemporaneous literature called Ah Wah) was hired for $900.00 to be interpreter and to write letters to Chinese contractors for ditch work (Morrison n.d., Rand 1974).

In the letter dated October 5, 1870, Pope told Foster of his sale of his interest in the Petrie and Bronk ditch in September to Fisk, who had traveled to Portland (Court Case 488):

> Portland Oct. 5, 1870
> Mr. C.M. Foster & Co.
>
> Dear Sir,
>
> I received from Wells Taylor & Co. a package of dust said to contain $200.00 then was the

amount at 16 per oz. I could not get but 15.25 per oz. for it therefore, a loss. I have sold the ditch to Mr. Fisk subject to the agreement with the chinamen made by you. I am well satisfied with my trade, as I get coin instead of dust at discount. I have given him an order on you for whatever you may have in your possession pertaining to Smalley and Popes affairs.

Yours Respectfully,

T. A. Pope

Either just before Fisk went to Portland or just after he returned, Charley Ah Wah told Foster that Fisk wouldn't let him [Charley Ah Wah] have anything to do with the ditch. It appears that Pope, in his mind, did not give Foster power of attorney to sell his share in the ditch (or he changed his mind without notifying Foster) and that Fisk, in his mind, now felt that he owned 1/2 interest in the Petrie and Bronk ditch.

Fisk apparently asked for all the documents relating to the Petrie & Bronk ditch that Foster had in his possession. During the 1870 Court Case, in deposition, Foster was asked about this during cross-examination by Defense Counsel:

> Question: You say you got an order from Pope to deliver up papers contracts in relation to the ditch to Fisk or words to that effect. Did you so deliver them?
>
> Answer: I did not. Only a portion.
>
> Question: What portion did you deliver?
>
> Answer: I think I gave him the mortgage that Pope and Smalley had on the ditch and power of attorney that Pope had given Smalley and there

might have been some other papers. I told him I wouldn't deliver to him all the papers belonging to the property for Pope had sanctioned my agreement with the chinamen and had received money on the contract and that he was acting in bad faith in reselling interest to Fisk and ordering me to turn over all property and papers belonging to Smalley and Pope to Fisk. I further remarked to Fisk that if he had obtained a deed to Pope's interest in the property that he couldn't obtain a deed to Smalley's interest until the price was paid or my power of attorney revoked.

The month of October was an active time in matters relating to this mining area.

The Hogem Ditch company gave notice on 18 October 1870 that they were enlarging the Hogem Ditch (Petrie & Bronk ditch) to carry water to Hogem and Kooster. The Hogem Ditch Company was James Fisk, William B. Simonton, and Elmer Fisk.

Packwood claimed 3,000 inches of water from Eagle Creek to supply water to Kooster, Shanghai, and the Powder River slope mines. Packwood's claim was recorded 9 November; the Hogem Ditch Company's on 18 November (Jaehnig and DeFries 1987).

It appears the Fisk and company were in direct competition with Packwood and company to see who would first get water to the Kooster area. Judging from the evidence in the available records Fisk's scheme seemed to be to carry water through the Petrie & Bronk ditch to Goose Creek, then run a new ditch (later called the Hogem Extension) due east from Goose Creek and then down to the Kooster area. The Hogem Extension Ditch's mouth was just downstream from the Sanger Mine area, just north from a heavily placer worked area on the east bank of Goose Creek. J. L. Curtis, the surveyer of Union County, was one of the owners of the big mine at Sanger (Simerville 1986).

Sometime in January, 1871, Packwood, C. M. Foster, I. B. Bowen, and Ed Cranston, in a horse-drawn rig driven by John Furman, liveryman in Baker City, drove to the Kooster area to lay out a new mining camp. This became Sparta, named after Sparta, Illinois, the town where Packwood grew up (Morrison n.d.; McArthur 1974). The Chinese had worked as contract crews on the Auburn Ditch and the Eldorado Ditch, both Packwood projects. The major crew on the Eldorado Ditch was the Ah Fat Company. This company did the bulk of the work on Packwood's Sparta Ditch (Gehr, Nelson and Walke 1978; Rand 1974).

Letters, written by Charley Ah Wah, were sent out in February, 1871, by the Eagle Canal company requesting Chinese crews for ditch construction.

On 7 April 1871, an injunction was filed against James H. Fisk and William B. Simonton:

> In the Circuit Court of the State of Oregon for the County of Union, Charles Ah Wah, Ah Chung and Ah Ming plaintiffs vs James H. Fisk and Simonton.
>
>> Whereas, an application for, an injunction order restraining the defendants from the use, control, and occupancy of the mining, ditch or canal, described in the complaint filed and submitted and from the use and disposal of the waters thereof; and whereas an undertaking in the sum of one thousand dollars has this day been submitted herein and approved in manner and from prescribed by law. It is therefore considered that the said application should be granted and it is ordered that the defendant

James H. Fisk and William B. Simonton, their
agents, servants, and all others acting through or
under them be and thereby adjoined and
inhibited from using, controlling, and occupying
the mining ditch or canal described in the
complaint and known as the Petrie & Bronk
Ditch, situated in or near Eagle Creek Mining
District, County of Union, and State of Oregon,
and the said defendants, their agents, servants,
are also further restrained and inhibited from
using, controlling, or disposing of the water of
said mining ditch or canal. It is further ordered
that this order remain in full force until further
notice of the court herein. Dated in Chambers of
the Dalles, Wasco Co., Oregon the 6th day of
April 1871.

In his deposition, 20 April, 1871, John Bates stated that
"said Fisk has now about 25 men employed to construct and
extend said ditch from Hogem to Kooster some 25 miles at a
great expense." He further stated that the injunction was
promoted by Packwood to harass Fisk and to delay the ditch
extension work so that "Packwood and company can
monopolise and control the price of water in the Kooster
District" (Court Case 488). Early in May the final ditch line of
what was then called the Packwood Ditch was staked,
construction contracts let, and the work started (on 11 May).

On 23 May, in two orders written by Judge L. L.
McArthur:

(1) injunction was dissolved and the order appointing
    the receiver was dissolved, and;
(2) the ditch was restored to the possession of Fisk and
    Simonton, and J. H. Shinn was appointed Referee to
    take testimony in the case and report his findings to
    the court at its next term.

On 16 July 1871, W. H. Packwood, J. A. Packwood and his wife, and Alexander Stewart sold to the Eagle Canal Company of Union County for $500.00:

> a certain canal and water ditch located in the fall of the year AD 1870 by Wm. H. Packwood and running from Eagle Creek and conveying three thousand (3000) inches of waters thereby to the Shanghai Kooster and Powder River Slope mines in Eagle Mining District Union County Oregon.
> Also a small ditch taking water out of said Eagle Creek below the above described ditch one same conveying water from said Eagle Creek to a point in said county Saw Mill (Book A, Deeds, pp: 597).

Then on 23 August 1871, E. Smalley, by his attorney in fact C. M. Foster, sold to W. H. Packwood, Rufus Perkins, Ira B. Bowen, E. P. Cranston, for $1.00, 1/2 interest in ditch and 1/2 of "a certain Board House situated in the town of Hogem " known as the Pope and Smalley store (Book A, Deeds, pp 619).

One day later, on 24 August 1871, Rufus Perkins, W. H. Packwood and his wife, J. A. Packwood, E. P. Cranston and his wife, A. E. Cranston, and J. B. Bowen and wife Ann Bowen mortgaged to James H. Fisk, for $1500.00:

> a certain water ditch . . . from Eagle Creek . . . to a mining camp known as Augusta or Hogem . . . said water to Bogus [sp?] Gulch and other gulches . . . known as the Petrie and Bronk water ditch and water right. . . .

this note to be due on or before 1 July 1872 (Book A, Mortgages, pp: 352).

Then, on 26 August, the attorneys for both sides filed

the following document:

In the Circuit Court of the State of Oregon for the County of Union.

Charles Ah Wah et al, Plaintiffs

vs

Cha. H. Fisk et al, Defendents

Suit in Equity

It is hereby stipulated that the above entitled suit be dismissed and that each party pay their own costs herein incurred.

And it is further stipulated that if any dispute arises upon the generation of costs that the same shall be submitted directly to the Judge of this court for his decision and the same shall be final.

Dated at Baker City Oregon August 26 AD 1871

S. O. Sterns
Atty for the Plaintiffs

J. D. Haines
Atty for James H. Fisk
Et al Defendents

At about this same time, late August, Fisk tried to create problems for Packwood by telling the head of one of the Chinese contractors that Packwood would never pay them as he could not complete the ditch. Packwood met with the Chinese contractors, convinced them things would work out, promising that he would put more men on the job in order to get all the rock work and flume construction done in time to handle the water running through the ditch. More Chinese were brought in, estimated around 300 total, and the progress of ditch construction increased (Morrison n.d.).

The Packwood ditch was complete 14 October, 1871, an event noted in the newspapers of the time.

> Now water is flowing in some of the principal gulches, and the hardy men who have appropriated the country look forward with certainty to a remunerative season next year. The two towns of Gem and Sparta are building up rapidly by substantial businessmen and an atmosphere of confidence, energy, and enterprise pervades the community.
>
> Twelve miles from Gem, over a good mining country just being opened, brings us to Hogem. The Hogem placer mines are about exhausted (Bedrock Democrat, 25 October 1871).

Water ran in the ditch and was sold until November. The going price being 25 cents per square inch for 10 hours and 40 cents for 24 hours. The Eagle Canal Company could earn, at a maximum, about $320/day of operation (Morrison n. d.).

On 22 April 1872, W. H. Packwood, J. A. Packwood and his wife, and A. Stewart sold to the Eagle Canal company for $500.00:

> and formerly known as the Petrie and Bronk water ditch . . . said property having been sold to Wm. H. Packwood, R. Perkins and J. B. Bowman and E. P. Cranston on the 23rd day of August AD 1871 by James H. Fisk . . . (Book A, Deeds, pp: 760)

While the Sparta Ditch was being constructed, the

Chinese workers comprised two-thirds of Sparta's 1,500 population. When Sparta's population peaked at 3,000, the Chinese accounted for one-third (Gehr, Nelson and Walke 1978). Water was a scare item, especially in the Blue Mountains during the summer months. Long ditches were constructed to move the water to the placer works utilizing Chinese labor by Packwood and Company who recruited from the Boise area. The Auburn Ditch was finished in 1863; a ditch in Rye Valley in 1864. The longest ditch, The Eldorado Ditch, ran 100 miles from the headwaters of the Burnt River to the placer area in Malheur County near Willow Creek (Dicken and Dicken 1979). The Sparta Ditch was 32 miles in length.

The Camp Carson Historic Mining District

Historic mining activity started in 1864 with the first activity on Tanner Gulch at the upper end of the Grande Ronde River. Eventually miners spread into several areas. Today we can identify two distinct mining activities, each focusing on a different type of mining process, placer mining and lode mining. We are only going to discuss the placer mining as this is where the Chinese were employed. At the upper end of the Grande Ronde River there is a vast placer mining region with three recognizable areas: 1) the Camp Carson Historic Mining District; 2) the Limber Jim Mining District; and, 3) the Rainbow Mining District. On the opposite side of the Grande Ronde Valley there is a small clustering of mining activity in the Pawnee Gulch Mining Area.

Much of the following discussion will illustrate the mining and business practices of the time. While this is more detailed information that any of the other areas discussed, the author suspects that it was fairly typical in all the mining areas regardless of the state including the lack of acknowledgment of the Chinese miners and especially the laborers that constructed so much of the support structures for these activities: ditches, flumes, dams, etc. The white miners apparently were as much interested to buying and selling claims as a profit motive as they were in doing actual mining.

Placer mining for gold started almost simultaneously with the first settlements in northeastern Oregon. Yet while there is a great deal written and known about the communities of the region, our knowledge of one of the main economic activities of the earlier period of local and regional history is almost nonexistent, primarily due to the sparsity of written records relating to the event. What few records exist, exist as newspaper articles and the surviving County Courthouse records of claims and deeds.

Gold mining stimulated the beginnings of the first permanent settlement of eastern Oregon. Settlement into this region began in August and September, 1859, when it was reported by W. W. Chapman, Surveyor General of Oregon, that emigration from the Willamette Valley, California, and from the Atlantic States was tending toward the region between the Cascades and the Blue Mountains, with more than a hundred settlers reported to have entered the Grande Ronde prairie.

By the fall of 1861, settlement had started on the floor of the Grande Ronde Valley. This establishment of settlements reflected the early economic impetus of the mass migration of men and materials to and from the gold mines. This is clearly reflected in the following statement made by Mr. Benjamin Brown, credited with being the founder of La Grande:

> When in November 1861, we were bringing in supplies and my family, we learned certain facts which gave direction to all our plans and put a brighter coloring upon the future of our settlement. We met, in the Blue Mountains, a

party of prospectors who had struck gold in paying quantities in Griffin's Gulch, near the spot on which the town of Auburn afterward stood. Their spokesman, who I think was Dave Littlefield, gave us great encouragement, telling us we were striking it rich [in building the settlement].

Gold mining also served to initiate: 1) the first developments in local road building; 2) cattle raising; 3) farming; 4) lumbering; 5) a context for Indian-White relationships; and, 6) Chinese immigration into the local area (Oliphant 1968; Mead 1974, 2006).

Placer mining within the Camp Carson Historic Mining District may be visualized as a series of high activity periods of time interspersed with periods of little activity. These high activity nodes may be seen as the following:

1863	Tanner Gulch placer activity
1867-1870	J. D. Reed - Tanner Gulch and the Reed Pit (located in the Upper Gravel channel)
1872-1875	James Carson - Upper Gravel channel (now called the Carson Channel)
1894-1900	Societe Minere - Tanner Gulch and Carson Channel
1916-1931	Turner Oliver - leasing "Camp Carson"
1940-?	Oroplata Mining Co. - dredging the river
1980-1983	Royal Western Mining, Inc.

The first activity in Tanner Gulch was essentially a

one-season involvement which established the fact that there was gold in the upper reaches of the Grande Ronde River. This pioneering activity planted the seeds for the future miners/entrepreneurs but little is truly known about this first event other than the following statements:

In regard to early history of Camp Carson, I had talk with Mr. Samuel Williamson. Mr. Williamson is quite elderly but his mind is clear as to early dates and history. He was a boy, about thirteen, when Camp Carson was discovered. His father was a highly respected pioneer whose homestead is part of La Grande now. This is the story he gave me: in the fall of 1862, two men, Doty and Kilgore, killed an elk on what is called Tanner's Gulch now. They dressed the elk there and one man taking his cup from his belt dipped up some gravel to look at the sparkling rocks. In this cup full of gravel he discovered some gold nuggets. These men came to Grande Ronde and camped by our home. They told the story to my father and showed him the gold. In the spring of 1863, father Thomas Williamson, my brother Joe Williamson, Mr. Tanner, Joe Larbe and Mr. Hatfield took a whip saw, tools and provisions and went to Tanner's Gulch on snow shoes by way of Starkey. They dug a pit and sawed lumber, put in a flume and made a ditch to the gulch. They mined about six weeks that fall and brought out $4,000.00 worth of course [sic] gold.

Brother Joe became ill and died in June, 1864, and father could not leave home so he sold the two shares to the other two men for $2,000.000, bed rock pay. That fall when these two men came, they paid the $2,000.00 to father and went to Walla Walla to spend the winter, and perhaps their money. One man was killed there, another was drowned in the Umatilla River that spring. That ends my story. (Oliver 1927).

A slightly different version of this tale fills in some of the apparent confusion as to the numbers of individuals involved.

In the late fall of 1862, two men, a Mr. Doty and Mr. Kilgore, riding horseback through the mountains looking for a shorter route for wagon trains from Powder River to Umatilla, killed an elk at this point in the river (now known as Tanner's Gulch). They dressed the animal and made camp. One of the men, going to the stream to wash, unhooked his tin cup from his belt, drank, then, ever on the lookout for signs of gold, dipped up a cup of gravel and to his surprise, found several small pieces of gold. They came down to the settlement at La Grande in a few days, and camped by a settler's new log cabin for the night. They showed him the gold they had gathered and told him where it was to be found. They had very urgent business in Portland and wished to get there before winter set in over the mountain passes so went on their way. Early next spring a party of five men took tools, whip saw and provisions and went up the river on snow shoes. They found the gulch, sawed boards and made flumes, built ditch and dug a pit and washed out $4,000.00 worth of gold dust. During the next year, two of the partners died, a third had a serious illness in his family and sold his share to the other two (Davis 1960).

The following version of this event is taken from a newspaper article.

In 1862, two men killed an elk in the place, now known as Tanner Gulch and sampled some gravel, finding gold color. They came to the Grande Ronde Valley and showed the gold to a pioneer, Williamson, and in the spring of 1863, four men - Williamson, Tanner, Larbo and Jim Hatfield - went to Tanner Gulch and brought out approximately $4,000 worth of gold in about six weeks.

This discovery precipitated a small stampede from Sumpter gold camp and other gold camps with miners packing in over the Elkhom range by animal trails.

J. Calvert of Baker, now is his 80' s, told Howell that several hundred thousand dollars of gold was washed out by hand from the overflow of the high channel and Tanner Gulch (*La Grande Evening Observer,* 30 March 1939).

Following this account there is a gap in what few historic records survive. The early, and the bulk of the mining activity in the district, was placer mining. These systems processed the gold-bearing deposits by running them through sluices to extract the gold. Placer operations require water, lots of water. Therefore, a major activity of the placer era (certainly the one requiring the greatest amount of capital) was that of building ditches to collect and carry the water to where it was required. By 1867, considerable placer activity must have been underway as sizable ditch building was in progress.

In 1867, a group of Chinese who were working the mine, conceived the idea of bringing water from Anthony Creek, between Mud and Anthony Lakes, and convey it to the Grande Ronde watershed to the location of the mine which was on a hill above a water supply. The long ditch was completed by the Chinamen after fearful hardship. They carried their supplies up the hill in the most primitive way, with their load balanced on each end of a stick across their shoulders. After their canal had been built, farmers in the North Powder water shed refused to let them divert their irrigation water and their ditch was useless (Hug 1961).

In no other accounts of Chinese ditch building activity in this region are there indications of free-lance construction such as that suggested here. One suspects that only after the farmers became irate did the non-Chinese miners, who most likely organized the activity, give the credit to the laborers, leaving them holding the bag, so to speak.

Around this time the first local newspapers made their debut and often printed short articles on the mines and mining activity in the area.

"From the Grande Ronde River Mine"

Mr. John Clarey, an enterprising miner from Grande Ronde River, has been spending a few days in La Grande, as a delegate from that new precincts to the Democratic County Convention. From him we learn that fifteen miners wintered on the river the past season. He informs us that some new and very rich discoveries have been made on Deadwood Gulch, and also in the hills near the river. A company proposes bringing water on the hill during the summer, and when that is accomplished there will be work for a great number of miners. Mr. Clarey says there will be sixty or seventy white miners employed in the camp during the summer, and a great many Chinamen. We should have a good wagon road to these mines at an early date (*Grande Ronde Sentinel*, 2 May 1868).

From Matt Rice, who has been on a visit to the
head of the Grande Ronde River, we learn that
the miners are busy at work, and a great many
are making money. As soon as rain sets in we
shall have good news from the camp. The boys
will winter in La Grande (*Mountain Sentinel*, 24
October 1868).

From these accounts we can see the mining activity
starting to move up Deadwood Gulch toward the Limber Jim
area and the continuation of mining around, most probably,
the Tanner Gulch site(s) with an unknown number, "a great
number," of Chinese suppling the bulk of the labor.

It would appear that there was a fair amount of travel
to and from the mines during this period as judged from the
following advertisement (*Mountain Sentinel*, 1 August 1868):

Duncan House Grande Ronde River Mines

This house is supplied with everything
obtainable and parties visiting the mines either
for business or pleasure can rest assured of
having every attention paid to their comfort.

J. G. Duncan

Around 1870, J.D. Reed found the upper gravel channel,
later named the Carson Channel, and ground sluiced for two
or three years after extensive ditch construction. This spot was
of large enough size to be subsequently called the "Reed pit"
(Klubusichy n. d.). It may well be that it was Reed who was
behind the ditch building activity of the "Chinamen"
mentioned earlier at the Anthony-Mud Lake sites.

By 1872 there appears to have been a major shift of
focus from Tanner Gulch to the upper gravel channel. This

"upper" channel runs north and east across the region and is more easily worked near the tops of the slopes than in the creek bottoms although a number of small operations processed the creek beds over time. It was during this time that the general area received the name "Carson" or "Camp Carson" with which it would be forever after labeled.

Grande Ronde Mines. These mines are located on the Grande Ronde River, about fifty miles from La Grande, in a northwesternly direction. They are limited in extent, but rich. The want of water had heretofore been the chief cause of the undeveloped condition of those mines, but now capitalists having secured them it is expected that large amounts of the "root of evil" will be captured. The ground has been the property of various persons, but the chief owners were S.B. Story and John Doran, who placed their interests in the hands of W.B. Crane, the owner of the copper works in this county, for sale. He succeeded in making a sale in a brief time to Messrs. James Carson of Michigan and S. W. Clark of Salt Lake, men of large capital. Mr. Crane, whose energy keeps him so constantly on the move that we were unable to see him, and these gentlemen arrived a few days since. Purchases were immediately made and men employed, and work is now actively going on. The capital controlled by the purchasers will enable them to bring water in the mines in such quantities that the most approved methods of scientific mining can be successfully adapted by them (*Mountain Sentinel*, 19 October 1872).

Last summer Messrs. W. B. Crane & Co. Sold their copper-mine and smelting works, located about twenty-five miles northeast of Baker, in Union County, to Messrs. Carson, Williams &

Co., of Detroit, Michigan. Crane & Co. also sold to the same company hill-diggings, with a 60-foot bank of gravel, situated on the head-waters of Grande Ronde River, in Union County. The new company at once put on a large force of Chinamen, and continued work until cold weather, bring in a ditch from the river to the hills. They will resume work in the spring on a large scale with Chinamen and hydraulics, and expect a heavy yield (Raymond 1873).

It was that sale, to James Carson, that ever afterward named the placer activity area as: Camp Carson. For a number of years it was noted in McArthur's Oregon Geographic Names that this was an old military camp as shown on a map of military camps in Oregon. The authors of this map assumed Camp Carson indicated a military installation because of the name alone. This error on the part of McArthur was corrected by the late Ben Francy, then District Archaeologist on the La Grande Ranger District, Wallowa-Whitman National Forest, who sent to McArthur a copy of the newspaper article and pointed out the Camp Carson was a miner's camp not a military camp. This illustrates how "history" sometimes comes into existence and can be quite erroneous.

Two years later all sounded well with the operation in the placer area.

Camp Carson - From P. A. Mahaffey who has just returned from Camp Carson, we learn that W. B. Crane is pushing ahead with the Carson Mine and that everything looks very favorable for a good clean-up this fall and the prospects are very favorable for the future (*Mountain Sentinel*, 12 September 1874).

The next year was also active.

> Mr. Reed, superintendent of Carson Mines on Grande Ronde River reports about 20 men employed and the prospects for the summer run highly encouraging. Mr. Hall of the same place was also in town and gives a like report (Mountain Sentinel, 20 June 1875).

Little information is available about the Carson operation in detail although a stray newspaper article indicates that the operation did all right.

> Pat Quade, a well-known miner and mountaineer of considerable experience, came down from the Carson mines last week and made things lively among the boys. He has been engaged in mining in the Grande Ronde River for about three years, and he says he has "as good a thing as he wants." He reports mining prospects at Camp Carson very flattering, and has no doubt large amount of money will be annually taken from these mines for many years to come (Mountain Sentinel, 20 November 1875).

Activity continued on into 1876 but it is unclear exactly which mines are being discussed.

> Charles La Bur, one of the proprietors of the new gold mines, left for San Francisco Tuesday morning to purchase the necessary implements with which to work the mines (Mountain Sentinel, 23 December 1876).

On 20 October, 1879, J. D. Reed filed a mining claim "one mile in length and ten rods wide running from this notice up Clear Creek, taken as an extension to the George Starkey

Tunnel Company, situated in the Grande Ronde river mining district" (Union County Courthouse, Mining Claims, Book A). A few years later, in 1881, J. D. Reed, J. H. Hunter, J. R. Ladd and Arthur Warnick established a claim about three miles below Camp Carson on the Grande Ronde River, one marker at the end of the tunnel on the river known as "Ladd, Warnick, Reed & Hunter tunnel" (Union County Courthouse Records, Mining Claims, Book A), platted on 26 September 1883 and resurveyed on 22 July 1887.

The following newspaper account give some insight into activities in the mining area.

> Grande Ronde Mines – From the La Grande *Sentinel* we learn that new mines have been discovered in that locality. The *Sentinel* says:
> Last week we made mention of these mines, based upon tumor. Since then S.B. Story called upon us and gave more particulars and corrected an error or two in which we were led. We stated that Carson and Clark were the owners, in this we were mistaken, the owners being Messrs. Crane and Clark, the former being the active Superintendent. The former owner of the ground purchased was Mr. Story. The surveys have all been made and give great satisfaction to Mr. Crane. Facilities for water cannot be excelled as the supply is obtained from never perishable lakes. There has been already 290 rods of flume track graded and one and three-fourths of a mile of ditch - five feet at bottom, seven at top and two feet deep - completed. The facilities for dumping at these mines, Mr. S. Informs us, cannot be excelled. When Mr. Story left the mines there was five inches of snow on the ground, but proved no impediment to the fifty Chinamen and four white men engaged on the work. In a few days we expect further particulars regarding these mines (Idaho Signal, Saturday, November 16, 1872).

After this there is an apparent lull in the historic records until 1893/1894. Then the following account appeared in the local newspaper.

> J. B. Thorson and Lon. Corbett returned last night from Camp Carson, where they have been doing development work on their mining property, and report the outlook promising. They very much favor the proposed road up the Grande Ronde River and say that the city will receive help from parties in that locality (La Grande Gazette, 9 March 1894).

This was the precursor of a major event in the history of the placer mining activities in the Camp Carson district although the initial newspaper accounts hardly gave an indication of what was to come.

> Pacific Northwest -- Fourteen of the principal placer claims, along the Grande Ronde River have been syndicated and it is expected that interested person will arrive at La Grande, Oregon in a few days to examine them with a view of closing for the entire lot (Mountain Sentinel, 29 March 1895).

Unmentioned by the newspaper account was the sudden spate of mining claims being recorded at the county courthouse in 1893/1 894 by the following miners: F. S. Smith, J. R. Smith, A. Curtis, C. L. Fox, J. H. Hunter, J. E. Foley and wife, H. P. Campbell, C. L. Meyers, Joseph Woosnick, Elam Harnish, Albert Lasell, Thomas Marcum (also spelled Marcom, Morcom, Mercom), Paul Buzinni, George P. Wilt, J. A. Ulsh and wife, D. K. Keltz, E. Williams and wife, and H. A. Bums. While there is no direct evidence to indicate it being so, it does appear that this nest of enterprising miners had caught wind of the rumor, or saw signs of investigations, that a French group was interested in the Camp Carson area. For this same group of miners, during a very brief period of time, recorded and then recorded again, a sizable number of claims during which they appeared to be straightening out the boundaries of these same claims. Much of this was done on the same day in the county courthouse.

It appears that many of the existing mining ditches had been abandoned (the old Reed and Carson sites) as these were also claimed as well. In October of 1895 all of these claims were consolidated by these miners into a single parcel by selling each of the claims to C. L. Fox and E. C. Harnish (two of the group) for a dollar per claim.

Shortly thereafter the following article appeared in the local newspaper.

"THE BIG MINING DEAL"

"Grande Ronde Placers In Possession of Purchasers"

The sale of the Grande Ronde placer claims, concerning which there has been a great deal said during the past summer, is now an accomplished fact and the company has taken normal possession of the property in pursuance of orders cabled from France. The property includes twenty-seven claims, or 540 acres of placer ground, lying contiguously and extending a distance of five and six miles along the Grande Ronde River. The property is purchased by a syndicate of Paris capitalists which will be known as the Grande Ronde Placer Mining Company. The amount of the purchase price is not stated, but it is known that the claims were held by the former owners to be of an average of about $2,300 each, and it is not likely that a much smaller amount was the purchase price.

Mr. Thomas Marcum, a mining man who promoted the sale, has been appointed as superintendent of the property, and extensive improvement on the same will be commenced at once. A contract has been awarded to Messrs. Hunter and Fox to put in a sawmill of twenty-five horsepower. The mill is to be put into operation at an early date, and the engine and boiler for the same has already been purchased. There is also now on the way a large quantity of pipe, giants and other mining material. Among other improvements in the way of putting the property in shape for work will be an electric light plant with arc and incandescent systems. There will be six arc lights placed at proper locations along the river, and during the spring months the mines will be operated both day and night.

The machinery and improvements are to be put in condition for operating at the earliest possible date. A large force of men will be employing during the fall and winter months in cleaning out and repairing ditches and in the construction of several miles of flumes. Three or four giants will be put to work on the start at the upper part of the claims. During the spring months there will be a sufficiency of water to operate continuously night and day and the superintendent expects to establish a system of reservoirs at the Grande Ronde and North Powder lakes by which the property can be worked at all seasons except during the freezing weather of the winter months.

Mr. Marcum will make his headquarters in La Grande during the coming winter, but will build a residence at the mines. Other buildings will be put up and in fact the superintendent's headquarters will soon assume the proportions of a small town for which it is expected a post office will be established.

There is now no doubt that this sale of the Grande Ronde placer property is one of the most important and extensive mining deals ever made in eastern Oregon, both in the way of the purchase price and the extent of the operations to be inaugurated. The company will spend many thousands of dollars in improvements and the operation of the mines will be continued for an indefinite time. Mr. Marcum stated that every claim was thoroughly prospected before the purchase was made, and every test known to scientific and practical mining was resorted to, and every result proved most satisfactory. He says the ground is of such an extent that it cannot be worked out in a century. This great mining enterprise means much for La Grande and the surrounding communities. A great amount of money will be expended for labor and supplies, and it brings home to every citizen the fact that no time should be lost in bringing that district into communication with La Grande by means of a well improved road, and one that can be traveled at all seasons (*La Grande Gazette*, 1 November 1895).

The newspaper account was somewhat premature as the sale wasn't actually recorded until 30 July 1896 when the following transactions took place:

1. C.L. Fox and E. C. Harnish sold the entire package of claims to E. L. Giroux and Thomas Merceux;

2. E. L. Giroux and Thomas Merceux sold the entire package of claims to Frederick Wood, an

attorney in La Grande;

3.   Frederick Wood sold the entire package of claims to the Societe Minere Des Placers De La Grande Ronde, office in Havre, France (often called the French Syndicate in subsequent accounts).

This transaction was handled through the Farmer's and Trader's National Bank on 6 August 1896 for $51,000. The Societe Minere ran under the corporate name of Grande Ronde Placer Mining Co., and had up to 200 men working for them (WHPC 1902b).

This was the first time a large scale mining parcel had transferred hands in this district. While the exact boundaries shifted around, from time to time, the total property became a commodity to be bought, sold, or leased, from this date (1896) until fairly recently.

There are no contemporaneous records other than the few newspaper accounts indicating exactly what the Societe Minere did, or how much they earned from their endeavors, but there are a few indirect suggestions.

> A gentleman who has just returned from a visit to the Grande Ronde Mining Company's properties on the Grande Ronde River, is enthusiastic in his praise off the thoroughness of the work being done there by Superintendent Morcom. He says that Mr. Morcom is a man who understands his business and has secured the services of men who are equally well-qualified.
>
> The mill machinery has been put into place and as soon as the lumber can be sawed the machinery will be enclosed. The mill will soon turn out lumber enough with which to cover the

electric plant, built a hotel, bunk house and several residences, among which will be a handsome cottage especially designed for the superintendent.

As yet the mines have not been worked, but as soon as the ditches and flumes are completed a good force of men will be put on and the yellow metal taken as rapidly as possible. This gentlemen says the mines are very rich and the French syndicate who has just purchased them and are preparing to work them on an extensive scale will unquestionably realize handsomely from their investment (*Bedrock Democrat*, 9 December 1895).

On the head waters of the Grande Ronde River in the southwestern part of the county placer mining is being carried on a most extensive scale by a French syndicate who recently secured a large scale tract of valuable ground. This company is yet to make its first clean-up, but there is little doubt that it will be satisfactory. There is much other placer ground in this section as well as a number of promising quartz ledges (*The Weekly Republican*, 12 September 1896).

A force of about eight or ten men is at work at the big placer mines near Woodley making preparations on a more extended scale than ever for next seasons work. The main supply ditch has been increased nearly one-third in size and an additional pipe will be put in operation on Carson Hill. Another pipe will also be worked in Tanner Gulch. The tunnel through the backbone of the hill, which is being constructed under control of private parties, has been reached a length of 275 feet and lacks but about fifty feet of being completed. On the Tanner Gulch side a new ditch and head-gate has been constructed. It is estimated that the capacity will be increased fully one-third over what it was during the past season (*The Weekly Republican*, 14 November 1896).

The post office at Woodley was established 1 February 1896 and discontinued by 30 November 1896. Woodley was named after Frederick Woodley. It is reported that the town(?) was a two-story hotel, an assay office and a sawmill, operated by Woodley (McArthur 1974; Barklow 1987:261). A map, ca. 1900, of the area shows a Superintendent's office and a post office at Woodley with an old steam mill and stables below in the flats. The Bill of Sale between The Societe Minere and J. E. Foley in 1900 describes Woodley as "the dwelling house, fence, stable, office and store building." In a 1939 mining prospectus (Anon 1938) it was stated that:

> This syndicate spent a great amount of money in preparation for mining operation, and had the property thoroughly tested and examined by both American and French engineers, and as a result of these examinations, they made extensive improvements on the property, including the digging of long water ditches into the Grande Ronde drainage, the building of a dam on Grande Ronde Lake, the construction of dwelling houses, shops, electric power plants, sawmill and other permanent necessities and improvements. This was all done by wagon road as the only means of transportation, and the ground was extensively hydrauliced [sic] for several years thereafter.

It does appear as if the Syndicate was here taking claim for all the ditching and dam building probably utilized long before they arrived on the scene and the fact that these structures were mostly likely built by the Chinese laborers that were working in the earlier placer mining activities.

Later in this same prospectus it is suggested that one of the reasons for the eventual termination of the French syndicate was their rather elegant approach to mining (Anon 1938):

> I have been informed that the French syndicate kept an elaborate office in Paris, officials traveled between Paris and the mine, there was a considerable staff at the mine, each of the staff had a servant, a stable of fine horses was kept for the staff, also other extravagances not compatible with American placer mining.

In Barklow (1987) it is noted that:

> The big building at the mine was beautifully furnished, with a lovely big chandelier above the table. There were large pillars on each side of the steps going down into the living room, where the large fireplace was. The owners of the mine had the finest of everything. They had lovely fringed-topped surries and prancing horses to pull them.

One receives the distinct impression that the Societe Minere built a large number of structures as part of their operation. Later transfers of the property list a sizable collection on the property. As we shall see later, none of the subsequent owners seemed interested in putting money into the property, but appeared mainly concerned with seeing how much they could extract from it. The main result being a slow deterioration of the property from the turn of the century until ca. 1920-1930's.

Table I lists those items that the Societe Minere were probably responsible for constructing (although some could have been left over from the Camp Carson days) with those items mentioned in the newspaper accounts indicated with an asterisk. Table I was constructed from a listing as part of a 1918 transfer of the property. No data has yet been found that indicates that there was any additional construction between the period of ownership by the Societe Minere and the 1918 property transfer. In 1916 Woodley stood empty and abandoned (Barklow 1987).

TABLE I - SOCIETE MINERE STRUCTURES

    No.4 Steam Pump
*   6" Giant
*   Flume 36' x 54" x 850'
*   3" Giant
    18" Pipe - 1200'
    11" Pipe -600'
*   Mining Generator with:
        a. Westinghouse Compound Excitor;
        b. Pelton Wheel (65 hp) w/oil generator.
*   Bunkhouses (2)
*   Boarding House (Hotel?)
*   Superintendent's House and Office (7-room house)
*   Officer's Quarters
    Separating Plant
    Blacksmith Shop
    Carpenter's Shop
    Barns (2)
    Machine Shop
*   Sawmill (25 hp) with Boarding House Cook

House

In 1898, the Societe Minere bought five additional claims from T. Lake, Eliza Lake, Irene Imhaus, John L. Rand and N. E. Imhaus. These claims had been filed that same year on Little Clear Creek from near "the waste gate of the Carson Reservoir" stretching 6600' north along the creek. An interesting point to be made here is that some of the individuals staking claims and then selling them to the Societe Minere either had positions or contracts with the organization, i. e.:

> Thomas Marcum - Superintendent at the mine
> N. E. Imhaus - A Manager of the Societe
> C. L. Fox and J. H. Hunter - Builders of the sawmill.

Later accounts stated that the Societe opened up two large pits. They moved approximately a million and a half yards of gravel, realizing approximately $500,000. A newspaper account (*Evening Observer*, 30 March 1939) suggested that the Societe Minere took out "over $300,000 in gold from the big French pit." The tailings from the French pit were washed into Little Clear Creek; those from the Little French Pit (Borman and Reed Pit) went through a tunnel in the rim rock into Tanner Gulch (Oliver 1927; Howell 1938).

In 1900 the Societe Minere bought additional claims from T. Lake and J. L. Rand. Then in the county courthouse records, 24 September 1900, is a statement that the Societe Minere "now in liquidation appoints N. E. Imhouse a manager as its true and lawful attorney" and "Maurice Taconet of Havre appointed by the debenture holders of the same society" to handle their affairs in France. Just prior to this, on

17 September 1900, the Societe Minere had sold its holdings to J. E. Foley who, with N. E. lmhouse, on 18 August 1903, sold the entire package of holdings to Foley, Imhouse and Company corporation. The Societe Minere had originally bought twenty-seven claims. By the time of the 1900 sale the property encompassed thirty-four claims.

Over the next few years there were a number of transactions, buying and selling the property and additional claims, but little indication of actual mining activity on the ground itself. Then, in August 1903, the following account appeared:

> W. H. Hazel, a mining promoter of this city, who has been in the east since last December, returned from Boston yesterday morning. While in the east Mr. Hazel succeeded in interesting a number of large capitalists in the Camp Carson mining properties. These men will send a force of workmen and prospectors to the mines at once and Mr. Hazel leaves this morning for Camp Carson to superintend matters. N. E. Imhouse of Baker City, who with his wife and daughter arrived in the city yesterday, is also interested in the deal made by Mr. Hazel (*Morning Observer*, 9 August 1903).

It was about this time that the Foley, Imhaus and Company corporation sold the claim package they were holding to the Carson Hydraulic Mining Co., soon to be renamed Carson Hydraulic Mining, Ltd. Then in the same year J. E. and Mary Foley, J. M. Ferguson and T. H. Williamson, and N. E. and Irene Imhaus sold additional claims to the Carson Hydraulic Mining, Ltd.

One week later another newspaper article seems to indicate that the company coming into the area had big plans and high expectations.

W. H. Hazel, a well known mining man on this coast as been secured by the recently organized syndicate of New England capitalists, who have taken hold of the big Carson placer mines up Grande Ronde, to take personal supervision of the work. Mr. Hazel is now in the city making preparations to go to work immediately. This has been the best gold producer for years up the river and thousand of dollars have been taken out in the past. It was the intention of the company to have commenced earlier in the season but it was impossible for Mr. Harlow Foss of Barton, Vt., an old California miner to visit these mines sooner. He spent several days looking over the property and is well pleased with the outlook. The mine comprises over 1,000 acres of rich ground and it is the intention of Mr. Hazel to commence higher up than has heretofore been worked. The working of this mine on a large scale means much to this city, especially superintended by a man with such a reputation as Mr. Hazel enjoys. He is enthusiastic over the proposition and feels confident in making it a great mine (*Morning Observer*, 15 August 1903).

In 1908, Foley, Imhaus Co., sold all their holdings to E. A. Stephens, who with his wife Carrie C., sold their package to the Grande Ronde Mining and Power Co. (E. A. Stephens - manager).

In 1910, the Grande Ronde Mining and Power Co., had 14 of their claims resurveyed and made 35 new placer claims on adjoining land.

Another sheriff's sale, this time in 1913, sold the Grande Ronde Mining and Power Co., to H. A. Shropshire. In 1914, the now named Camp Carson Mining and Power Co., bought the Indiana Ditch and its water rights from W. A. Wilson and Frank Turner. H. T. Harvey and Annie Harvey were listed as the owners of the Camp Carson Mining and Power Co. They sold the entire holding back to H. A. Shropshire, who in turn mortgaged it to Turner Oliver, who hired Gordon Land to be his Superintendent.

Turner Oliver bought the Camp Carson Mining and Power Co., at a sheriff's sale in 1916. This appears to be the beginning of a new era in the region, one of leasing.

T. Oliver leased the property to a number of operators who worked, or planned on working, the claims. In 1917 a one-year lease was made with Paul Denhart. The Circuit Court in 1918 affirmed the sheriff's sale to Oliver. The next year, 1919, Oliver gave a long lease (1919-1924) to Doan, Sims and Darby Co., who subleased to the Alto Vista Mines Company. Alto Vista apparently couldn't fulfill their sublease as Oliver, in 1921, leased the property to W. M. Rose and L. M. Duncan, both of Portland for the years 1921-1931. They subleased to the World Gold Syndicate (L. M. Duncan, president; G. Evert Baker, secretary) who in turn subleased to the Rose Gold Concentrator, Inc., Company. This group apparently worked the claims as a report by Remy (1926) mentions "a power house built by the present owners" in Tanner's Gulch. However, it would appear that overall the property had begun to deteriorate as it was noted for this same year that the Carson Ditch was bringing water to camp but the Clear Creek and Grande Ronde ditches needed repairs. Water to work the placers was available from three sources: Grande Ronde Lake, 20 acres; Grande Ronde Meadows, 50 acres, and; Carson Reservoir, 20 acres.

In 1926 it was also noted by Remy that on Little Clear Creek there was a 30 inch flume, 500 feet long, with angle iron riffles in the lower end and a 2 1/2 inch giant connected to 900 feet of steel pipe. Leading from the French Pit there was a four foot flume over 1200 feet long in fine condition. At the lower end of the property there was a small sawmill with a two-story, 11-room house and five other cabins (which sounds very much like the description of Woodley).

In 1938, Anna Oliver leased her properties to Harry T. Howell who overhauled the ditches, pipes and roads and built a penstock at the mine (County Courthouse Mining Records).

The next year another flurry of activity took place with a renewed interest in working the placer deposits at the Camp Carson claims.

"Thars gold in them there hills" is the sentiment of Harry T. Howell, general manager of the Carson Channel Gold Syndicate of Spokane, who arrived Tuesday from Spokane with a truckload of supplies, equipment and men.

Howell accompanied by five men, reports he is leaving the latter part of this week for the high channel of Camp Carson, located in the Blue Mountains of Union County, 30 miles west of North Powder, to start spring developments on the mine. He hopes to be washing gold out by the early part of May.

"Camp Carson is one of the largest placer mines in the United States," asserted Mr. Howell in his discussion of the mine. "I have been up there the last three years testing the ground and have satisfied myself it can be put on a big producing basis," he continued. "Over half-million dollars were taken out of Camp Carson in the early days. There is a total of 30,000,000 cubic yards of gold gravel in the channel." From Howell's prospectus is the following brief resume of the camp's history.

In 1862, two men killed an elk in the place, now known as Tanner's Gulch and sampled some gravel, finding gold color. They came to the Grande Ronde valley and showed the gold to a pioneer, Williamson, and in the spring of 1863 four men - Williamson, Tanner, Joe Larbo and Jim Hatfield - went to Tanner Gulch with equipment and brought out approximately $4,000 worth of gold in about six weeks.

This discovery precipitated a small stampede from Sumpter gold camp and other camps with miners packing in over the Elkhom range by the animal trails.

J. Calvert of Baker, now is his 80's, told Howell that several hundred thousand dollars of gold was washed out by hand from the overflow of the high channel and Tanner Gulch.

In the 70's a Mr. Reed prospected around the top of the high channel and opened the Reed Pit. Reed died shortly after his discovery and the pit has never been worked since.

A Mr. Ferguson visited the Camp Carson mine in 1936 and reported to Howell that he had been a miner from 1890 to 1905. In 1890 a Mr. Church was general superintendent of the mine for some La Grande mining men, but due to Church's inexperience he was unable to save the small gold.

Later the mine was taken over by the French company and Ferguson was given the job of foreman. They worked the mine from 1892 to 1895 and washed out over $300,000 in gold from the Big French Pit. Then, due to financial troubles, the outfit, with offices in Paris, shut down.

In May 1936, Cushing Moore (now deceased) and Howell examined Camp Carson placer mine for 10 days and found an enormous body of good commercial gold gravel.

Howell has had over twenty years experience in this work as a hydraulic operator. On June 1, 1936, a 60-year lease was secured from Mrs. Anna Oliver, of La Grande, for the property.

Howell is transporting his men and equipment to the camp via the winter road through Starkey. By May he plans to use the summer road which goes through North Powder (*Evening Observer*, 30 March 1939).

This is an interesting article in that it clearly illustrates how the history of the Camp Carson area was already being distorted by the passage of time. The operating dates for the Societe Minere are wrong and one wonders about the comments relating to Reed who was alive and working for the Societe Minere and probably sluicing out his old pit as well.

The Camp Carson placer mines near the headwaters of the Grande Ronde River in Union County, Oregon, will be in full operation again this season. For the past two years Harry Howell of Spokane, Washington, has worked the property.

In that time he has proved to his satisfaction that there are values and yardage to justify working the ground on a much larger scale. For the purpose of carrying out these plans Mr. Howell is at the property getting work started with a crew of men.

His plan is to take advantage of the spring flood waters piping with a 6inch monitor. With the dead work to be done before piping he plans to be in full operation in the fore part of May, and will have water to run until about the first of July.

Following that he will start the work building dams for storage reservoirs and digging new high-line ditches to carry water for hydraulicing. When this is completed he will have one of the largest hydraulic mine operations in the west.

Camp Carson is one of the better known early day placer mining districts in Eastern Oregon. It was worked more than 40 years ago by a French company.

Associated with Mr. Howell in the enterprise are a number of Spokane mining men. His address is at North Powder, Oregon.

Mr. Howell is going to the mine by way of Starkey from La Grande. He has a caterpillar tractor to bulldoze the snow out of the road about nine miles from Starkey. Later in the year he will go over the mountain road to North Powder which is several miles nearer (*Eastern Oregon News*, 31 March 1939).

Fred Chrisman of North Powder is leaving this week with a crew of men to begin the 1940 season at Camp Carson hydraulic gold mine at the head of the Grande Ronde River. The crew was organized by E. J. Mimnaugh of Spokane, president and manager of the Carson Channel Gold syndicate, operators of the property for the second season. The manager will return in mid-March to stay for the season.

According to estimates, the company has opened about 30 million yards of gravel in the channel with approaches 1900 feet in width. The gravel is said to contain values from 30 to 50 cents per yard and can be mined for 5 cents. They have 50 claims on royal purchase from Mrs. Oliver of La Grande, and last year installed 1400 feet of pipe and raised a 300 foot earth dam in Turner Gulch to regulate water flow through the mile of ditch. They operate with two 5-inch giants. Water for the six month operation is available in the river.

Equipment being taken in includes a Denver mineral jig, to recover gold sulphides in

Fred and Lilian Chrisman of North Powder, Oregon, worked at Camp Carson in 1939-1940 with Lilian working as the cook of the camp. About eight other individuals also worked at the mine during this period. During their stay at least one of the buildings in the main Carson cluster was falling down and pieces of the "hotel" were being removed. Fred mentioned a dump which he covered over with the camp dozer as a way of cleaning up the area. The company was first run by Harry T. Howell and then by Gene Mimnaugh. The mine was operated as early in the Spring as water could be run in the ditches. It ran until mid-August, at which time the water became limited. One person was employed full-time to pull the overburden out of the sluiceways. The sluiceways were cleaned about every two weeks. The reservoir held enough water for about one shift of work (Chrisman interview with Francy).

The year 1940 was a year of activity in the gold mining region. By the end of 30 June 1940, the Carson Channel Gold Syndicate, Inc. (E. J. Mimnaugh, president) had undermined and cut down 10,000 yards of gravel, spent ten days driving it through sluice boxes, built a reservoir and dam, installed 1000 feet of pipe from the penstock to the Reed Pit, installed two giants, built a new intake at the head of the Grande Ronde ditch, built new flumes and installed a hydro-electric plant (Union County Courthouse Records).

A big gold dredge started working on the
upper Grande Ronde River yesterday afternoon. It

will eat its way along the riverbed 24 hours a day, seven days a week for the next four or five years, turning out a solid gold brick every two weeks, according to the plan of the Oroplata Mining company.

La Grande is supply headquarters for the dredging operations, which will employ about 20 men the year round. A little village of eight houses, a bunk house, commissary, and sheds has been erected in the last two weeks for the workmen and their families.

The dredging site is about 13 miles above Mt. Emily camp, the last five miles over a road which the mining company itself had to build. It is near the old Indiana Mine and intercepts Muir Creek, from which hundreds of thousands of dollars in gold were washed in hydraulic operations years ago.

It is the biggest mining operation in the county.

The company was formerly located at Granite, in Baker County. Its new location, although only 17 miles north of Granite, necessitated moving the machinery and equipment about 150 miles. The dredge was "knocked down" and hauled in pieces, some loads weighing more than 30 tons. Twenty-seven men have been employed during the move.

With the beginning of operations yesterday, the company went on a permanent threeshift, seven day schedule, working under floodlights at night. With about $150,000 invested in the machinery, officials explained, it is necessary to operate full time in order to keep costs low enough to make a profit on the comparatively low-grade deposits.

S. K. Atkinson, president and general manager, and J. E. Tucker, secretary-treasurer, are in active charge, S. K. Atkinson, Jr., is superintendent of the dredge.

The dredge, which is floating on a little pond which it keeps moving along, hauls in about 450 cubic yards of gravel and rock a day. It washes out the free gold particles, dumping the gravel out the back. After about two weeks of washing, they have a "clean-up" day, when they gather all the gold out of the ripple boxes in the form of an amalgam with quick silver. It is then heated in a retort, evaporating the quick silver and leaving pure gold (*The Observer*, 24 September 1940).

The last and totally non-productive attempt at placer mining spanned the years 1980-1983 when a company, Royal Western Mining, Inc., made an attempt to revitalize the old Camp Carson pit and work the lower deposits. After three years, having filled in the Reed pit and creating a mess that took the Forest Service years to stabilize, they declared bankruptcy and abandoned the mine and their equipment.

A Chinese Village in Camp Carson Mining Area

Two Dragon Camp, named by the archaeologists working the site rather than the original inhabitants who left no written records of their stay, located in the headwaters of the Grande Ronde River of northwestern Oregon, is a Chinese settlement reflecting traditional Chinese cultural values and world view.

The site appears to be unique in that the bulk of the heavily documented archaeology of Chinese habitation sites have been, for the most part, urban setting within the towns of the Far West (LaLande 1981). This village was occupied seasonally as winter, during the time period, in the Blue Mountains at or near 6,000 feet elevation, would, and did, disallow a year round occupancy for anyone. It appears that this village, as we called it, is unique as the literature dealing with the Chinese in the mining regions makes no mention of anything like this occurring elsewhere. So, the question becomes one of:

why did these Chinese laborers do this, build a small village way out here in the forest?

One part of the answer is that this spot is perfect *feng shui*. It is nestled between two ridges lines, one curved and one straight, in the swale between them with a small stream running through the middle of the spot which is in turn edged by the curving mining ditch which had flowing water passing by and headed ultimately to the placer mining activities, all aspects of the best kind of *feng shui*.

The Chinese practice of *Feng Shui* is "a complex blend of sound common sense, fine aesthetics and mystical philosophy. Based upon topographical and architectural features, this practice aims to ensure happiness and prosperity via harmonious relationships" (Walters 1988).

Unlike Western civilization, which tends to establish a mediator (God) between humans and their surroundings, the Chinese believe that the cosmos is self generated and perpetual. There is no reliance on the will of a deity; there are no gods to serve or placate. Rather, principals are based on self-evident propositions that regulate the universe. Comprehension of Heaven and Earth is felt to be "the great root" or "the great foundation" of living. The relationships of man and the regularity of the cosmic order are felt to be as one. Men are not considered to be unique in the universe, but rather as part of it, their ultimate goal being the achievement of harmony with nature. *Feng shui* is a medium of social interaction. It interrelates the idea and the values of the community to the social practices and the metaphysical settings and symbols of the culture (Lung 1978; Feuchtwang 1974).

One goal of Chinese culture was to have all things in harmony with their surroundings on the assumption that if this was true then happiness and prosperity would naturally follow. Occurring in the landscape are mystical entities which men may harm or improve, weaken or strengthen. One can change the landscape so that it no longer will have the same affect and to bring it into a more positive direction. *Feng shui* is the unifying set of principles based upon the analysis of the formation of the landscape and the means of how to properly align oneself to these features for a proper harmony and balance. It was a way of conceiving and of perceiving realty as well as a way of dealing with that reality. *Feng shui* is considered to be a natural phenomena that is all encompassing and the ultimate cause of both social and natural events. It is primarily concerned with orientation in physical space, itself considered a natural phenomena (Feuchtwang 1974).

Feng Shui was first compiled by the scholars Yang Yun Sung, who was the Imperial Geomancer, and Tseng Wen-ti in the 9th century in the province of Kuang-Hsi (Kan-chou) in Southwest China. Then known as The Forms School, it was a geomantic form of divination utilizing lines, figures and portents shown by the earth. Four centuries later, the Compass School was founded - a divining approach much like *feng shui* although it places a greater emphasis upon elaborate formulae and schemes, taking into account every conceivable directional, astronomical, and calendrical implication. It was founded by Wang Chili in the 11th century and was also called the Fukien School as it was started in north Fukien. By the late 19th and early 20th centuries the two schools had merged somewhat although the mountainous areas of south China tended to favor the Forms School.

Feng Shui was based upon the human response to the forces working in the cosmos. It began with natural phenomena, spatial relationships, related them to metaphysics and then to social aspects/events. Landscape is believed to affect humans directly, in the ideal case to make them feel relaxed, content and confident. The abstract goal of *Feng Shui* is to ensure that all things are placed in harmony with their surroundings, after which it is assumed that happiness and prosperity will naturally follow (March 1988; Walters 1988; Lung 1978; Feuchtwang 1974).

Chinese philosophy involves an assortment of elements that weaves a perspective together; the all encompassing aspect being "Ta" or "the Road," "the Way." Man's standard is considered to be the Earth; Earth's standard is Heaven, Heaven's standard is Tao, and Tao's standard is spontaneity. The Chinese consider the greater whole to be divided into complimentary and opposing components, the duality being expressed by Yin and Yang, (Female and Male, Dark and Light). In addition, there are Five Elements or Natural Forces that govern both natural and human events via their respective periods of rise and decay. The Five elements of a site must be taken into consideration and are identified as follows: Wood - tall cylindrical features (visualized as trunks of trees); Fire - sharp peaks; Earth - flat, eroded terrain; Metal - rounded hills; and, Water - wavy undulating ground (Waters 1988). Any visitor to the site (Two Dragon Camp) can identify these elements in the skyline and surrounding terrain of the village.

The Chinese believe that the constant motion of the stars and planets gives notice of the changing events of the universe both on and outside the earth. The earth itself dictates the situation in which humans find themselves. Each individual is subject to the twin influences of the Heavens and Earth. Where the heavens are understood through astrology, the earth is understood through *Feng Shui*.

Literally *Feng Shui* means "Wind-Water." It stands for the power inherent in the natural environment as well as the entire cosmology of metaphysical concepts and symbols. It is a school of thought based on the belief that everywhere there are currents of invisible energy, or "Cosmic Breaths," that constitute the virtue of a site. They are blown about by the wind and held by the water. If the wind is high, the Breaths will disperse; if the water moves fast, the Breaths will be drawn away (Freedman 1966; Feuchtwang 1974).

Both beneficial and malign currents exist, called *ch'i* and *sha* respectively. When investigating a site, any possible *sha* have to be identified. *Sha* currents go straight and are favoured by sharp edges, usually of artificial origin, such as canals, roads, ridges of roofs, edges of buildings. Streams or other water courses pointing at a site are also believed to be carriers of these fatal currents. It is therefore important that a building not stand in the path of any straight lines. Even more ominous is "The Secret Arrow," a hidden pointer created by a sharp bend or angle in a river or in the fabric of a building. Under no circumstance should these be seen to point to a door or window. Fortunately, *sha* can be blocked or deflected by trees, walls or ornamental features.

Ch'i, however, meander along irregular paths and are favored by curved surfaces. They are carried by the continuously descending paths of streams. Once water has passed by the site, it should no longer be visible, as it is otherwise believed to carry off essential *ch'i*. Nor should windows open onto the downstream of a river.

In order to ensure concentration of the Cosmic Breaths, a favorable thing to do, the key features of the site are having a "Dragon" and a "Tiger" in a proper relationship to the site proper. A Dragon is seen as a hill rising above the others, one slope rising sharply, the other falling away. That is, the ridge might be referred to as a dragon's back. It is regarded as a beneficent force. Where there is a true dragon, there must also be a tiger, a curved rise with lower and gentler slopes. The tiger is regarded as a force of danger which protects only as long as it is in a complimentary relationship with a dragon. Ideally, the Dragon and Tiger will be "in embrace;" being a pair of hills forming a horse shoe or bow shape or a pair of cupped hands.

An ideal *feng shui* site would be formed like an armchair, comfortable and protecting. There will be hills to the rear, supporting, giving strength, and warding off evil spirits brought in by cold winds from that direction. There will be hills flanking the site like embracing arms; the Azure Dragon ideally placed to the East, Northeast or Southeast (or to the left as facing the open unshielded side), The White Tiger ideally located to the West or right. The front of the site is always deemed south, and everything that South stands for. The front is symbolically South even if the site must face in some other direction, and being so, it should always have an unhindered view. The front will be open or unobstructed so that airiness and sunlight can be brought in by the yang spirit. The back is always North and should be blocked. The left is always East, the right always a symbol of West (Freedman 1966; Walters 1988; Feuchtwang 1974).

True dragons are found in the aspects of the undulating landscape. And just as Dragons and Tigers in the mountains generate terrestrial ch'i, flowing water may do the same thing. These Water Dragons have much the same impact on a site as do the True Dragons. Streams, water courses, flowing east-west are regarded as favorable. Shape is also critical as well. Gentle curves are considered as the most favorable, with straight lines being the most negative (Walters 1988).

Other considerations when laying out a site include avoiding obstacles in front of the house as they are regarded as extremely bad omens. Trees to the back side, however, are regarded as auspicious since they protect the house from unfavorable winds. These trees should have plenty of foliage, evergreens are considered to be the best of all. Pine trees are a symbol of virtue and longevity. Finally, care of the trees is vital; it is important not to scar or damage *Feng Shui* trees in any way.

The salient features in the environment are those which can be traced as lines: watercourses, ridges, or those which have definite shapes: mountain peaks, pools and ponds, large boulders or other natural features (Feuchtwang 1974).

Another part of the reason for the placement of this Chinese village must be in the fact that this spot is about three miles from the placer activities and from where the white miners lived. While it is a very easy walk from the village, along the ditch berm, to the mining areas, it is too far for the rather casual harassment, especially at night, as often seen elsewhere between white miners and the Chinese. Doxiadis (1970) states that there is only one factor which defines the distance that anyone wants to go or can go in the course of daily life and that is the method that one utilizes to do this. The limit of the rural dweller, or in this case The Chinese laborers, as a pedestrian is around one hour, approximately three miles for horizontal movement. This puts this place at the far edge of that distance and makes this, for the most part, a peaceful and isolated spot. The Chinese mining camps in many of the mining areas were often purposefully located away from the other miner's camps hoping to lessen the potential for hostile acts (LaLande 1981).

Tentative dating for the site is ca. 1870 - ca. 1890. The inhabitants were probably involved in the construction, or reconstruction, of the several placer mining ditches that fed the main activity areas of Camp Carson, and perhaps with other aspects of the placer mining activity itself. A tentative estimate of population size, based on 4 individuals x 26 structures, suggests a resident population of around 100 individuals, more or less.

Pirazzoli-T'Serstevens (1971) stated that in the ancient Chinese cosmology, which considered Heaven as round and Earth as square, space is imagined as a series of squares within squares. Square, in the Chinese sense of the term incorporated what in Western culture includes the terms: square, rectangular, etc. An analysis done by myself, during the seven years of investigation of this village, on the "squares" of Two Dragon Camp and all those other "squares", that is, cabin remains, scattered throughout the La Grande Ranger District, Wallowa-Whitman National Forest, by loggers, ranchers, non-Chinese miners, and others, brought to light as interesting aspect of what square is. A plot made of the numbers representing the ratio (length to width) of the Chinese squares and the non-Chinese squares demonstrated as subtle difference in how space was visualized. The Chinese ratio had high clusters at the ratios 4.8, 6.1, and 8.1. The non-Chinese ratio had high points at 6.7, 8.6, with the majority at 1.0 (perfect square). These two populations of squares reflect the different cultural concepts of squareness.

After the 7+ years of analysis and work on the site, it was felt that the various aspects of *Feng shui,* reflected by the site location and the internal arrangement of the structures, clearly demonstrate that this site was a Chinese constructed, Chinese occupied camp, at least during its initial period of history. Given the large number of "structures" it was also felt that an estimate of 100 individuals is a very conservative guesstimate.

There were only 45 Chinese listed for Union County in the 1870 Census and 235 in the 1880 Census. Of the 45, 1870 Chinese, 36 were self-identified as "miner" and all were living in La Grande. These miners were most likely working in the mining areas of the upper Grande Ronde, Camp Carson being the main focus for such activities. By the 1880 Census all the Chinese miners listed for Union County were clustered in and around the mining areas of the far eastern edge, the Sanger and Sparta mining areas (Mead 1992, 2006). This strongly suggests one of two possible explanations for the Chinese population of Two Dragon Camp:

1) by the time the Census was taken, the

Chinese miners were no longer involved with mining in the Camp Carson area and the camp had been abandoned, or;

2) that they were still living at Two Dragon Camp but they were overlooked by the Census taker who did not know of their existence, or perhaps, did not care.

The inhabitants of the camp recycled various items which today would be heaved into the garbage. Cylindrical tin cans were modified for other usages. One was fastened to something else with two square nails. Another was given a wire bail and hung over a fire as the base shows heavy swelling and heat scaring/staining. A can base, was punched full of holes by a square nail, perhaps to be utilized as a strainer. Rectangular tin cans all have one or more nail holes punched just below the open end, just below the lip. Those with one nail hole may have been nailed to something, such as trees, for storage (?). Those with numerous holes may well have had wire bails added to them to serve a handles for buckets(?). Several clusters of cut pieces of metal were found which suggests that they were set aside for future use but never utilized.

The opium cans were cut into pieces. One of these pieces was turned into a funs tray, paraphernalia utilized when smoking opium.

One of the coffee pots whose handle was broken was repaired by utilizing a piece of wire to refasten the handle back in place.

The Chinese ceramic fragments found on the site, portions of a single bowl, were of the type manufactured in China for export. The major locations for these exports were the ports of Canton, Sawtow, Macao, and Hong Kong, in order of descending importance (all located in Kwangtung Province). The port of San Francisco was one of the major distributing centers of such items due to its proximity to the California gold fields and the major travel routes to the other more interior gold fields (Olsen 1978).

The single piece of non-Chinese ceramic on the site dates ca. 1890+ which may be an indication of minor reuse of the site by non-Chinese after initial abandonment by the Chinese.

The repaired rubber boots show the same sense of frugality as the recycling of the other materials on the site.

All in all, the feeling is of a population that is making the greatest use of all available materials in their day to day activities which is, perhaps, a reflection of the reasons that brought the Chinese here in the first place, i.e., to make money and send as much as possible back to the mainland.

Stenger (1992) suggested that all "rural sites so far examined . . . demonstrated nearly identical ceramic assemblages . . ." In addition to the apparent consistency there were co-occurring Japanese and Chinese wares. Based upon the artifactual assembly so far recovered from Two Dragon Camp, we have to suggest one of two things relative to Stenger's study.

1) Stenger's rural sites were a biased sample, that is, they are some sort of "urban" artifact assemblage, or,

2) Two Dragon Camp is an anomaly in that it appears to be the only Chinese village mentioned in the literature.

Given the state of the literature, we do not believe that there is a quick answer to this problem but wished to raise the point here in order to point out that the widely held and believed-in concept of a constancy across all Chinese sites may not be true.

The vernacular architecture on the site follows an interesting pattern of spatial subdivisions. Lung (1978) in his study of Chinese cultural space described the tripart subdivision of private dwellings in rural villages. He pointed out that they had three rooms. The central room was the kitchen, the back room was for sleeping and storage, and the front room was the more public area opening out onto the outside. What we can see reoccurring in the housing sites in Two Dragon Camp, which was in all likelihood an all-male, seasonal community hired for their manual labor, is a truncated rural village house. Each of the units so far excavated has a kitchen space and a sleeping/storage space with no need for the public third room as here, unlike life in the rural villages, there was no requirement for family privacy for here there were no families.

An interesting aspect of the work done by Lung (1978) was his realization that the several villages sites he was looking at were arranged in such a way across the landscape that their positioning was fixed by interesting "rules." Each of these villages were "square." When he projected lines draw diagonally from one square, or line projected from a corner through another wall's center point, these lines carried across the landscape would hit a corner or mid-point on another village square. In his study of the locale he was interested in, five villages were interconnected this way with lines radiating in such as way that all pointed at each other. Even though one standing on the ground could not see some of the villages from other of the villages.

During the analysis of this village, an accurate map was drawn. A year later, after reading Lung's work, similar lines were drawn from every square on the map. And every line draw from one square hit another square on a corner or mid-point of a side. Given that there are 26 "square" sites in the village, the occurrence of this is well beyond any coincidental happening or random event. One of the occupation sites had one corner anchored to a massive rock. Thus this site could not be moveable, that is, of all the sites in the village it could not have been organized from any of the others, so it appeared, to our eyes, that this was the first site from which all the others were "drawn" upon the landscape, the assumption being that one had to start somewhere in the overall organization of the 26 "squares" on the site. Regardless, the village certainly did not follow Western concepts of village planning (see Myers 1998 for an in-depth discussion of Chinese Vernacular Architecture).

Chinese Culture in Two Dragon Camp.
        A number of things that were seen inside the village gave us some small insight into the culture of the inhabitants.

The Wrong Way Tree
        Lying diagonally across the southern edge of the south-eastern corner of the site is a 140-foot long tree. This tree crosses over two of the features of the site. The stump of this tree is approximately 36-inches in diameter and from the angle of the bird's mouth cut into the stump, and the butt of the tree lying immediately adjacent to the stump, it appears that the intent was to fall the tree away from the occupation area. However, the tree fell 180 degrees from the intended direction suggesting that the tree was not properly cut. The only other explanation would be a rather radical twist to have occurred during the felling. It would appear, then, that the Chinese miners were marginally conversant with logging techniques.

Log Sources for Structure Construction
        A survey was run around the entire site in order to try and locate the source of the logs utilized in the several features. Thirty-four stumps were located that show the same type of cutting as the logs utilized in the several features. Based upon the survey, it appears that trees were fallen and then cut into the appropriate log length prior to utilization. In addition to the thirty-four deliberately cut trees, two trees that had toppled

from heavy winds at some point-in-time, leaving roots wads poking into the air, were also sawn into lengths and utilized. Two other trees still lay on the site, cut into lengths but not utilized. The trees show both saw and axe cutting. Stump diameters range from 14 to 36 inches.

It appears that most of the trees taken were already dead. In one feature, a wall log was utilized after it had already been burned on one side and may have been a lightning strike. In some cases, there are traces of bark on the logs which suggests either recent dead, or live.

Fire

From the presence/absence of charcoal we plotted the extend of a small ground fire. It started at the downhill southwest corner of one cabin, burned uphill along the south side of the structure, burning a deep gouge along the lower log at ground level before fanning out up the hill. From the burn pattern, and the scorching at the lower southwest comer, it appears that the fire started at this corner of the building and crept up slope. It also appears that the fire stopped of its own accord and was a very low intensity burn. This suggests that the ground was open with very little burnable materials littering it other than the normal forest duff buildup. It also seems a good assumption that given the number of probable occupants of the site and the number of cooking spots that all the handy woody materials on the ground would have been gathered and burned leaving the ground within the village rather clean of materials that would support wildfire. None of the trees inside the burn show signs of scorching or other fire damage. Judging by where the fire started it appears that fire was probably due to an unattended fire in the fire place from which it escaped.

Chinese Vandalism(?)

During the excavation of one of the cabins it became apparent, from the moment that the duff overburden was removed, that the interior of this feature had a large mound of dirt shoveled into it. At first glance it appeared as if someone had dug in the site and then thrown their waste materials back into it. However, by the time we reached the original, upper floor, it appeared that there had been no "free-lance" excavating by parties unknown searching for artifacts, but that someone had thrown all this dirt into the site without digging inside it. This was further confirmed as it became apparent that the stone feature at the west end of the site had been toppled before the dirt was thrown inside. Fallen wooden material was also buried under this "backfill." Lying downhill and between two of the living sites is a squarish depression. From rough measurements, the amount the dirt inside the backfilled site and the amount of dirt removed from this depression are the same. Under this thrown-in "back-dirt" lying on the floor, we found artifacts. It appears that there was deliberate vandalism to the west end of the structure with a subsequent shoving in of a large quantity of dirt. And the event appears contemporaneous with the original occupation of the site. As there were no signs of burning inside the feature, we eliminated the idea that this was an frantic attempt to put out a burning structure. In New Zealand, the Chinese invariably abandoned houses after a death or suicide had occurred (Ritchie 1986). Perhaps, this could explain the apparent "vandalism" here.

However, there does appear to be another explanation. Throughout the site there are a number of very large dead trees which appear to have been blown down at the same point in time.

These trees all measure around 100' tall. They are all pointing in the same direction which suggests a major wind storm toppled them during the same event. Each of the several "cabins" that had been filled in with dirt were one of the structures that one of these toppled trees had struck. Wind storms of this nature tend to occur in the winter when the heavy storms blow in from the south. Given the Chinese sense of *feng shui*, the suggestion is that when the miners returned in the spring they found these trees down and across a number of their structures. In order to restore the harmony of the site the struck areas were filled in with dirt. It could also be, after the back-filling, that the village was abandoned as the fallen trees were an indication that the site's *feng shui* was no longer harmonious and the site no longer safe for habitation.

Southwestern Oregon

This corner of the state was uninhabited by Euro-Americans until the inrush of gold seekers who were a mixture of Mexicans, Chinese, Hawaiian Islanders, Europeans, and Euro-Americans. The Euro-Americans gained immediate political and economic control (LaLande 1981).

Gold prospecting had moved northward from the first California fields along the Trinity River in 1849, to the Klamath and Scott Rivers (1850), to the Shasta Valley (1851). In the summer of 1850 a few miners were working the placer gold deposits on the Illinois River in the vicinity of Josephine Creek (Dicken and Dicken 1979). Shortly after, during the winter of 1851-1852, a gold strike was found in Jackson County on the Rogue River, near the present site of Jacksonville, on the place owned by Alonzo A. Skinner at Rich Gulch. Other deposits were located along the Rogue's tributaries, especially the Illinois, the Applegate, and Bear Creek (LaLande 1981; Lyman 1903; Chen, L. 1972; Dicken and Dicken 1979). Jackson County had just come into existence on 12 January 1852 (McArthur 1974).

Scattered gold discoveries were made on the Burnt River and in the John Day Valley in 1853-1855. The mining town of

Susanville, Grant County (which was then still part of Wasco County) was established in 1854 and was named by a party of miners who had come to Oregon from Susanville, California (Hudson 1978; McArthur 1974). The northern California town, Crescent City, was the entry point for many of the Chinese heading for the Siskiyou Mountains in 1850 (LaLande 1981).

Shortly before 1855, a Chinese camp was located at Kerbyville, Josephine County (which was then still a part of Jackson County). By 1857, numbers of Chinese had moved into the southwestern corner of the state. A letter to the newspaper of the time complained about the Chinese that were engaged in mining.

> The Chinamen are about to take the county. There are from one thousand to twelve hundred in this [Josephine] county, engaged in mining. They are buying out American miners, paying big prices for their claims. (*Weekly Oregonian* (Portland), Oct. 1, 1857:2.)

However, the 1860 Census only listed 425 Chinese in Oregon, five of these being east of the Cascades and living in The Dalles. Jacksonville had a Chinese section of town called the "China Shacks," and the "Chinese Quarter" in the late 1850s (Barth 1964; LaLande 1981; Edson 1974; Spreen 1939). The largest nugget ever found in the mines was in 1859 on the East Fork of Athouse Creek by Mattie Collins, weighing two hundred and four ounces (Spreen 1939).

Beach mining began along the coast in 1861 on the beaches at Ophir, Pistol River, Gold Beach, Port Orford, Cape Blanco, Bandon, Old Randolph, and South Slough, between Coos and Curry Counties (Spreen 1939).

A company that was formed in 1864 to build a mining ditch from Squaw Lakes to a placer site apparently failed without doing the construction. Later, 1877-1878, The Squaw Creek Mining and Ditch Company hired Chinese workers to do then what had not yet been done, build the ditch. When they were finished, the company stated that "the Squaw Lakes Ditch Co. will hereinafter hire none but white laborers . . . No Chinese need apply" (LaLande 1981).

In 1879 the Grande Applegate Mining Company was organized by German Jewish merchants in Roseburg and Jacksonville to begin hydraulic mining on the west bank of the Applegate River about 2.5 miles upstream from its junction with Palmer Creek. Chinese crews built a 5-mile long ditch to supply water taken from a point near the mouth of Carberry Creek during the winter of 1878-1879 (LaLande 1981).

Gold was discovered on the Upper Columbia River in 1855 and along its tributaries. The general mining boom that developed in the northeast portions of the territory generated an enormous demand for food and all kinds of supplies and transportation. The economic heartland of Oregon, the Willamete Valley, and Portland, cashed in. The Columbia and its tributaries for almost 500 miles upstream from Walla Walla saw both white and Chinese prospectors (Wynn 1964). Wynn (1964) describes the route to these areas as being from Sacramento, through the Oregon goldfields in the Jackson/Josephine area, to the Snake River, and finally to the Clearwater or the Columbia. In all probability, this route would have been Sacramento to southwest Oregon (where nearly all the early gold finds were located, then north to Portland, up the Columbia, and then to the Snake or Clearwater. In 1855, eastern Oregon was essentially, to the non-Native Americans, a vacant and untraveled space.

The Constitution of Oregon, passed on 18 September 1857 (Oregon gained statehood 14 February 1859) included the clause:

No Chinaman, not a resident of this State at the

time of the adoption of this Constitution, shall ever hold any real estate or mining claim, or work any mining claim therein (Art XV, Sec. 8).

The legality of this section was never tested. On 5 November 1946, it was finally repealed (Edson 1974). It had been a group of Oregon miners who had pushed for their resolution that only American citizens would be recognized as holding claims in the state. This resolution was published and almost immediately adopted in all of the gold camps. During the writing of the California Constitution, it was the Oregon contingent, led by Peter H. Burnett, that pushed much of the essential features of the Oregon Constitution into California's constitution, including the Chinese exclusions (Lyman 1903). In 1880, the Circuit Court in California deemed this approach as being unconstitutional.

Jackson and Josephine Counties, also in the year 1857, enacted the Foreign Miners Tax in an effort to control the Chinese and/or pump money into the local coffers (LaLande 1981). This appears to be an idea brought up from California by the white miners.

By 1864, the region southwest of Jacksonville, called Upper Jackson Creek, was "almost exclusively Chinese . . . " In this same general area the Chinese tended to work in "companies," groups of ten or twenty that functioned as a unit.

Kaspar Kubli's store, opened in 1859 and located near the confluence of the Applegate River and Thompson Creek, was the main supplier of Chinese sundries during this period. The store obtained imported items from Tung Chong and Company, San Francisco. In the years 1866-1868 the store purchased $4,270 worth of merchandise, mainly food items, for resale. The average monthly food bill for their Chinese clients was around $10. The store, operated until 1872, had a clientele that was, in the main,

Chinese miners (LaLande 1981).

Gin Un, a Chinese entrepreneur, purchased and ran a hydraulic mining operation in the Little Applegate Valley in 1864, and in the 1870's constructed a 4.5 mile long ditch, The China Ditch. It is estimated that he earned about $2,000,000 in gold (LaLande 1981).

In Jackson County, the Sterling Ditch, 23 miles long, was constructed by Chinese "gangs" hired by white-owned placering companies on Squaw Creek and Sterling Creek. It was completed in 1877 (LaLande 1981).

The Chinese appeared to have been involved in most, if not all, the ditch building activities associated with the mining activities in Oregon as various of the placer mining districts formed water companies to construct ditches, or canals, to bring water to the placer works. One ditch, located southeast of Prairie City is still called China Ditch.

As the hydraulic mining after 1890 fell away the Chinese population faded. By the 1990 Census only 43 Chinese remained in Jackson County, twenty years later there were 30 (LaLande 1981).

Northwestern Oregon

The 1850 Oregon Territory Census listed only two individuals as having been born in China. One was a white logger who was working in Lewis County, Washington. The other was a servant, Ah Sing, working at the Vancouver Barracks. California at this time had a listed Chinese census population of 660 (Wynn 1964; LaLande 1981).

In 1851 when Portland was incorporated, it claimed a citizen population of 820 (with no Chinese) which was about the size of San Francisco before their gold rush. Shortly after Portland incorporated, however, the first Chinese of record, Sun Sung, opened a restaurant and boarding house (LaLande 1981).

When the first brick building was raised in 1853 the citizens rejoiced and set about removing the tree stumps from the unfinished streets. They had apparently been embarrassed at hearing visitors call Portland, "Stump Town." The city continued to grow: 1860 - 2,874; 1870 - 8,293; 1880 -17,577 (Paul 1982). Regular steamer connections were established between San Francisco and Portland also in 1851.

During the gold rush into the Northwest region, the western parts of Washington, that is Washington Territory, were bypassed. The area of Colville became the focal point for the prospectors of the Oro Fino gold deposits in 1860, then the Boise Basin further east in 1862, then the bars of Elder Gulch in 1863. The bar of the Columbia was worked in 1862 and 1863 with "hundreds" of Chinese along the river from Rock Island in 1864 (Wynn 1964).

Shortly after Oregon achieved statehood in 1859, the discovery of gold in 1860-1861, in and around Lewiston, started the migration of miners into and through eastern Oregon (Edson 1974; Barth 1964; Paul 1982). In 1860, the Oregon Steam Navigation Company was formed with an initial capital stock of $172,500. By the next year, 1861, the company had steamboats carrying freight three times a week from Portland to the Dalles for the eastern side of the state.

The Willamette Valley during the winter of 1861-1862 was devastated by heavy rains which inundated the valley floor washing away factories, mills, farmhouses, livestock, and fences. Hundreds left to seek economic relief in the gold fields (Spreen 1939). The mining rush for river traffic was so intense that the company reported carrying 10,500 passengers. The steamer *Okanogan* was paid for after its first trip (Spreen 1939). In 1862 the number of passengers jumped to 24,500, and by 1863 to 36,000 (Paul 1982). Steamboats were soon established on the upper Columbia to carry men and material the rest of the way although many traveled by foot or by horseback to the Blue Mountains (LaLande 1981). Portland became the distribution center for all the goods coming from San Francisco and the receiving port for all the gold coming from inland (Wynn 1964).

On 19 October 1860, the first mandatory state licensing law for the Chinese was passed. It levied a $2 per month tax on Chinese miners, a $50 tax on Chinese merchants. Ten percent of the money collected was to go to the state treasury, ninety percent to the country collecting the tax (Edson 1974).

Primarily due to the anti-Chinese agitation in California, the Federal Act of 1863 excluded coolie labor from immigration into the country. This, however, did not affect the population already inside the United States as they did not come to the U.S. under that system. An inspection of the average age of the Chinese population over the next thirty years suggests that this act had little affect of the Chinese population. The average age stayed relatively constant which suggests a rather constant leaving and returning to home of earlier immigrants and a replacing of that population by more recent arrivals.

By 1867 all of the United States was being affected by the post-Civil War economic slump which led to great and lasting tensions in the West between non-Chinese and Chinese laborers.

However, the business community saw things in a different light, much less threatening

> The steam communication which has just been inaugurated between China and San Francisco, promises not only as being beneficial to the latter town, but also to the interior country. Judging by all appearances, a large immigration from China may be expected, and mines in Oregon and Idaho, which have been played out, will be reworked by Celestials. An agent representing a large China company at San Francisco, has been sent to the Dalles with instructions to make this

point his headquarters for immigration. The agent
-- who of course is a Chinaman -- has already
leased a large house on the O.S.N. Co's bridge and
is having it refitted for a China hotel (*Washington
Statesman,* Feb. 8, 1867).

Chinese began entering through Portland directly from
Hong Kong in 1868 probably under the direct control of the
Chinese Consolidated Benevolent Society of Portland (Leland
Chin, president). An number of ships of various nationalities are
listed in the literature (Yu 1991) and the numbers of Chinese on
board:

> *Jeanne Alice,* French - 430
> *Edward Jones,* American - 380
> *Garibaldi,* American - 210
> *Alden Besse,* Spanish - 180
> *Forward,* British - 330
> *Manila,* ?? - 425.

The bulk of these laborers were contracted to the railroads
(Wynn 1964). Ben Holiday, who was building his railroad south
along the Willamette Valley towards the California & Oregon
Railroad which was building north from California to connect
with him, apparently took his cue from the Central Pacific
Railroad, and hired Chinese laborers. He contracted with Wa
Kee, a Chinese labor merchant, to bring them in shipload lots
(Clark 1974). When track laying halted in the mid1880s near the
present town of Medford many of the workers headed down to
the Siskiyou Mountain mining areas (LaLande 1981).

From 1866, when the first salmon cannery was established
by R. D. Hume at Eagle Cliff, Washington, the Chinese began to
work in the canneries. The canneries were established along the
Columbia River and in most of the coastal rivers and Bays,

including the Nehalem River, Tillamook Bay, the Nestucca, Siletz, Siuslaw and Umpqua Rivers, Coos Bay, and the Coquille and Rogue Rivers. Between 1876-1930, the China House located at the Warrendale Cannery on the Lower Columbia housed 30-80 Chinese laborers (Sullivan 1983). The preferred site for a cannery was on the shore near a good supply of water with the canneries being built on wharfs so boats could easily unload. The number of canneries began a steady expansion in the 1870's as the steam canning process, developed in Europe, allowed a better and more reliable packing process which increased the number of canneries to 39. The salmon pack rose from 10,000 cases in 1869 to 450,000 cases in 1878, making salmon the leading export item after wheat and flour. Most of the fishermen were Scandinavian and most of the cannery workers were Chinese. The Chinese were preferred because they would accept low wages; they would work long hours; and, they had no inclination to join labor unions. However, in 1886, probably under labor union pressure, the cannery operators informally agreed to replace their Chinese laborers with white laborers (Friday 1982; Dicken and Dicken 1979; Smith 1979).

The canneries had houses which had as many as 50 to 100 bunks under one roof. These were dubbed "rookeries" by local Astorians. Chinese boarding houses were built along the same line (Friday 1982).

However, while large numbers worked in the canneries or on the railroads, the Chinese were still working in the mining area.

> These people may be seen in numerous places
> working over many old diggings; and, along the
> bars of the Rogue River. . . in washing out the gold
> which white labor has neglected as too small pay.
> In some places they have large wheels, driven by
> the current, for raising water for their sluices (*The*

Oregonian, August 8, 1868).

Chinatowns, or densities of Chinese dwellings, developed in many of the small towns like Auburn, Clarksville, Humbolt, and Sumpter, in Baker County; Granite, Union, Prairie City, Mt. Vernon, Canyon City, and John Day, in Grant County; Sparta in Union County; Jacksonville, in Jackson County (Chen, C. 1972; LaLande 1981).

The Census of 1870 showed the distribution of the Chinese in the western states as follows: California 49,277; Idaho 4,274; Oregon 3,330; Washington 234. It was noted in 1870, in Portland, that Chinese servants were paid $30 month, but without any mention as to whether this was high or low compared to non-Chinese (Corbett and Corbett 1978).

An advertisement by the Kam Wah Chung Company (established in 1871) in the *Grant County News* read:

> Kam Wah Chung, contractor for Chinese labor.
> Laborers of all kinds furnished at short notice.
> John Day, Oregon.

Large numbers of Chinese began to migrate into the Lower Columbia Basin both from abroad and from the mining areas. Between 1875-1883 *The Weekly Astorian* recorded dozens of ships arriving with Chinese on board. They came from San Francisco and from Hong Kong. The primary attractions were the canneries and railroads, including the Canadian Pacific in British Columbia. Many times large numbers of Chinese were returning home, although this event was rarely reported. However, in 1887, two groups, 500 and 342, were reported as leaving the United States headed for China (Friday 1982). In 1870 44% of the Chinese population in the cannery region along the Lower Columbia (Clatsop and Columbia counties in Oregon;

Pacific and Wahkiakum in Washington) worked for the canneries. By the 1880 Census the percent had risen to 77.3% (Friday 1982).

The Weekly Astoria mentioned various aspects of the Chinese section of town in issues spanning 1876-1882. "Chinatown" was concentrated on the two streets closest to the canneries on the pilings over the swampy tidal flats. It had a number of stores and other establishments catering to the Chinese population including a Chinese theater (Friday 1982).

The Oregon horticulturist Seth Lewelling and his Chinese foreman Ah Bing working in Lewelling's orchards in Milwaukee created a new variety of cherry in 1875 which was named Bing. This was either because Ah Bing was responsible for the new cherry or was named after him for his long service (35 years) with Lewelling. Ah Bing went to China to visit in 1889 and could not return because of the Chinese Exclusion Act of 1882.

In 1881, the overall economic interactions of the Chinese laborers to the larger culture were observed and reported by Wallis Nash, an English visitor to The Dalles.

> The food, save the rice, is purchased in the State; the material of the clothes they wear is manufactured and sold in the United States; the tools they work with also. So that it is only the profit on their labor's price which goes to China; and some of that goes to pay their passage in the ships which transport them to and fro.

Nash also observed that there were about 500 Chinamen toiling on the railroad right-of-way cutting the rock near The Dalles (Edson 1974).

The years 1882-85 were the depression years with unemployment being severe in Oregon and Washington. The failure of the Northern Pacific Railroad in 1883 and the completion of the Canadian Pacific in 1885 caused a temporary halt in railroad construction with thousands of laborers becoming suddenly unemployed (Clark 1974).

Yet elsewhere the situation must have been different. In Baker City, a Chinese Joss House, a two-story structure finished inside with hardwood, was built in 1883. It cost $10,000. In their homeland the most prominent building of a village was the temple, called "Joss houses" by the whites. This term was a corruption of "Deos," a Portuguese label for God.

As the economic picture shifted in the counties through time, there was a gradual urbanization of the Chinese population as they drifted into those places where employment could be found. By the end of the century, Portland possessed the second largest Chinese population in the United States standing next to San Francisco as a major Chinese center (Chen, C. 1992; LaLande 1981).

Chapter Five

Chinese Occupations as Reported in the Oregon Census: 1860-1990.

The stereotypic image of the Chinese in the United States is a person who either runs a restaurant or a laundry.

In 1860, the first Census taken for the newly created state of Oregon, there were 425 Chinese listed. Of these, five resided east of the Cascade Range, in The Dalles. They were a cook and four laundrymen. By 1870, there were 45 Chinese living and working in Union County and 680 in Baker County. These numbers increased to 235 in Union County and 787 in Baker County by the time of the 1880 Census. In Union County, for both census years, 75% of the total Chinese population were listed as miners while for Baker County it ranged 87% and 81% respectively. In terms of the mining population, that is, all individuals listed as "miner" in the census tracts whether Chinese or non-Chinese, in 1870, in Union County 44% of all miners were Chinese, increasing to 84% in 1880. In Baker County, in 1870, 53% of all miners were Chinese, increasing to 64% in 1880.

The overall picture is one of large numbers of Chinese working as miners, increasing over time. Yet, when reading the contemporaneous literature, one rarely runs across any indication that they were there. The entire history for the Camp Carson district as presented earlier would leave one with the impression that there were few Chinese miners, which was hardly the case.

One writer in California in 1869 listed the following occupations for the Chinese: woolen factories, knitting mills, railroad building, highway and wharf construction, borax beds, farms, dairies, hop plantations, small fruit farms, kitchens, wood cutting, land clearing, potato digging, salt works, liquor manufacturing, cigar and cigarette making, the manufacture of slippers, pantaloons, vests, shirts, drawers, overalls, and shoes, tin shops, shoe blackening, fishing, gardening, poultry and pig raising, peddling, cabinet making, carving, whip and harness making, brickmaking, washermen, house servants, coal heavers, deck hands, cabin servants, sailors, mining, vineyard laborers, and laborers in the tule lands (Sandmeyer 1973).

As we have seen, the Chinese were in a number of other occupations. The following lists, for Oregon, in alphabetical order by County, were extracted from the Federal Census for the years 1860, 1870, 1880, and some of 1900. There is no detailed data for the year 1890 as the original protocols were destroyed by fire before they were microfilmed. As the various counties came into existence at various points of time the data is listed by the first census within which the county appeared. Recognize as well that various of the counties were hacked out of existing counties so that in one census the larger county would be listed and in the next the newly created county as well as its "parent" county would show. The date after the county name is the year that the county was created.

For those who wish to peruse Census microfilm there are a few things to keep in mind. The Chinese are often listed by their white-bestowed nicknames; John, Jack, Doc, etc (LaLande 1981). Clan names were hardly used within the family or a group of same named individuals which would be the same as always talking to someone and always using both their first and last name. The Chinese used the term "Ah" in place of the clan name. Census gathers assumed that this was part of the individual's name. Thus one may find Ah Jin, or Ah Charley, etc. (Palmer1972). In either case the true identity of the individual being listed is lost.

One other point to make. Do pay attention in the following lists and to the effect on occupations, type and total number, between the census dates 1880 and 1900. The exclusion laws where quite negative in terms of the varieties of jobs being filled after they were passed (1880s) and the number of occupations actually being filled.

Baker County (1862)

Female	1870	1880	1900
Prostitute	*	*	
Washing	*		
Domestic servant	*		
Courtesan		*	
Keeping House		*	
Pantry woman			*
Dress maker			*
Housekeeper			*
Male			
Miner	*	*	*
Restauranteur	*		*
Clerk in store	*	*	*
Cook	*	*	*
Laundryman	*	*	*
Doctor	*		
Interpreter	*		
Gambler	*	*	*
Keeps gambling house	*		
Gardener	*	*	*
Merchant - China goods	*	*	*
Shoemaker	*	*	

Farm laborer	*	*
Servant		*	*
Day Laborer	*	*
Physician	*	*
Sawyer	*	*
Merchant	*	*
Butcher	*	
Keeps wash house	*	
Tailor	*	
Minister	*	
Herder	*	
Teamster	*	
Opium dealer	*	
Farmer		*
Laborer - R. R.		*
Baker		*
Barber		*
Boarding house		*
Hog Dealer		*

Benton County (1847)

Male	1880	1890
Servant	*	*
Cook	*	*
Laundryman	*	*
Farm Laborer	*	*
Day Laborer	*	*
Sawyer	*	
Farmer	*	
Laborer - R. R.	*	*
Works in Brickyard	*	
Scavenger	*	
Ironer		*

Hog Dealer   *
Grocer   *
Restauranteur   *

> Note: there were no Chinese listed in either the 1860 or 1870 census.

Clackamas County (1843)

Female	1870	1880	1900
Keeping house	*		
Male			
Laborer-Paper mill	*	*	*
Laborer-Woolen mill	*	*	
Laborer-Factory	*		
Cook	*	*	*
Laundryman	*	*	*
Grubbing		*	
Laborer-Orchard		*	
Laborer-Nursery		*	
Day Laborer		*	*
Gardener		*	*
Boss Chinaman		*	
Weaver-Woolen mill		*	
Farm laborer		*	*
Servant		*	*
Woold dried		*	
Giger		*	
Sawyer		*	*
Potter		*	
Hop Grower			*
Keeping house		*	*
Ironer			*
Farmer			*
Salesman			*

Laborer-R.R.   *

Clatsop County (1844)

Female	1860	1870	1880	1900
Keeps House			*	
Housekeeper			*	
Servant			*	*
Dress maker			*	*
Seamstress			*	
Merchant				*
Male				
Restauranteur			*	*
Clerk			*	
Cook		*	*	*
Laundryman		*	*	*
Contractor			*	*
Fisherman			*	
Hotel porter			*	
Laborer-Cannery			*	*
Gardener			*	*
Merchant				*
Shoemaker				*
Farmer			*	*
Servant			*	*
School teacher			*	
Physician			*	
Dish washer	*	*		
Laborer-shoe factory			*	
Invalid			*	
Pawn broker			*	
Tailor			*	*
Tinsmith			*	*

	1860	1870	1880	1900
Baker			*	*
Carpenter			*	
Saloon Keeper			*	
Barber			*	*
Laborer-R. R.			*	
Butcher			*	
Grocer			*	
Day laborer			*	*

Columbia Country (1854)

Male	1860	1870	1880	1900
Cook			*	*
Laundryman			*	*
Laborer-cannery			*	
Laborer-mill			*	
Grubbing			*	
Sawyer			*	

Note: there were no Chinese listed in either the 1860 or 1870 census.

Coos County (1853)

Female	1860	1870	1880	1900
Wash woman			*	
Housekeeper			*	
Cook				*
Male				
Miner		*	*	
Cook			*	*
Waiter			*	
Laborer-saw mill			*	
Laundryman			*	*
Doctor			*	
Physician			*	

Day laborer	*	*
Dish washer	*	*
Merchant	*	*
Servant	*	
Salesman		*

Note: there were no Chinese listed in the 1860 census.

Curry County (1855)

Male	1860	1870	1880	1900
Miner		*	*	*
Day Laborer			*	
Servant			*	
Cook			*	*
Laundryman			*	
Engineer-steam				*
Laborer-cannery				*

Note: there were no Chinese listed in the 1860 census.

Douglas County (1852)

Female	1860	1870	1880	1900
Prostitute			*	
Washer woman				*
Male				
Miner		*	*	
Servant		*	*	
Cook		*	*	*
Laundryman			*	*
Laborer-R. R.			*	
Day laborer			*	*
Laborer-saw mill			*	
Dish washer			*	
Keeps wash house			*	

Note: there were no Chinese listed in the 1860 census.

Gilliam County (1885)

Male	1860	1870	1880	1900
Laborer-R. R.				*
Laundryman				*
Cook				*

Grant County (1864)

Female	1860	1870	1880	1900
Keeping house		*	*	
Laundrywoman		*	*	
Servant			*	
Chop house			*	
Baudy house			*	
Housekeeper				*
Male				
Miner		*	*	*
Merchant		*	*	*
Tailor		*	*	
Runs gaming house		*		
Butcher		*		
Doctor		*	*	
Cook		*	*	*
Druggist		*		
Huckster		*		
Baker		*		
Hotel keeper		*		
Clerk		*		
Restauranteur		*		
Runs boarding house	*			
Day laborer		*	*	*
Boot mender		*		
Laundryman		*	*	*
Physician		*		

	1860	1870	1880	1900
Gardener		*	*	*
Farm laborer		*		*
Carpenter			*	*
Sawyer			*	
Opium dealer			*	
Loafer			*	
Blacksmith			*	
Shoemaker			*	*
Hog pedlar			*	
Barber			*	*
Jewelry			*	
Gambler			*	
Shepard				*
Grocer				*
Priest				*
Stock herder				*
Servant				*

Harney County (1889)

Male	1860	1870	1880	1900
Day Laborer				*
Cook				*
Servant				*
Laundryman				*

Jackson County (1852)

Female	1860	1870	1880	1900
Keeping house		*	*	
Servant		*		
Male				
Miner	*	*	*	*
Cook	*	*	*	*
Day laborer	*	*	*	*

Keeping house	*	
Hotel keeper	*	
Trader	*	
Butcher	*	
Gambler	*	
Carpenter	*	
Tailor	*	
Barber	*	*
Doctor	*	
Keeps gambling house	*	
Artist	*	
Gardener	*	
Physician	*	
Servant	*	
Merchant	*	*
Runs boarding house	*	
Porter	*	
Waiter	*	
Laundryman	*	*
Runs China store		*

Josephine County (1856)

Female	1860	1870	1880	1900
House keeper		*		
Keeping house		*	*	*
Male				
Miner	*	*	*	*
Cook	*	*	*	*
Laundryman	*	*		*
Blacksmith		*		
Day laborer		*		
Physician		*		
Mule packer		*	*	

	1860	1870	1880	1900
Mule breaker		*		
Doctor		*		
Hotel keeper		*	*	
Butcher		*		
Gambler		*	*	
Servant			*	*
Mine boss			*	
Merchant			*	
Barber			*	
Farm laborer				*

Lake County (1874)

Male	1860	1870	1880	1900
Servant			*	
Cook			*	*
Laundryman			*	

Lane County (1851)

Male	1860	1870	1880	1900
Cook	*	*	*	*
Day laborer	*	*	*	*
Miner		*		
Washerman		*		*
Wash & iron		*	*	*
Domestic servant		*	*	*
Cook in hotel			*	
Section hand-R. R.			*	
Garden servant			*	
Wood sawyer			*	
House servant			*	
Washer			*	
Fireman on engine			*	
Laborer-sawmill			*	

Dealer in China goods				*

Linn County (1847)

Female	1860	1870	1880	1900
Keeping house			*	
Male				
Laundryman		*	*	*
Store keeper			*	
Laborer			*	
Cook in hotel			*	*
Servant			*	
Wash house			*	
Wash man			*	
Wood sawyer			*	
Farm laborer			*	
Cook			*	*
Domestic-house work			*	
R.R. section hand			*	*
Dish washer				*
Merchant-China goods				*
Physician				*
Day laborer				*
Farmer				*
Hop raiser				*

Note: there were no Chinese noted in the 1860 census.

Malheur County (1887)

Female	1860	1870	1880	1900
Prostitute				*
Male				
Cook				*
Merchant				*
Day laborer				*

Miner	*
China store/merchant	*
Shoe maker	*
Restaurant proprietor	*
Dish washer	*
Laundryman	*
Farm laborer	*

Marion County (1849)

Female	1860	1870	1880	1900
Keeping house			*	
Male				
Washer & ironer	*			
Washing		*	*	
Cook	*	*	*	
Laundryman		*	*	*
Convict		*		*
Servant			*	*
Wash dishes			*	
Laborer			*	*
Collector			*	
Saws wood			*	
Merchant-dry goods			*	*
Tailor			*	
Pedlar			*	
Contractor			*	
Merchant			*	*
Jobbing			*	
Druggist			*	
Ironer			*	
Clerk in store			*	
Barber			*	*
Grubbing			*	

	1860	1870	1880	1900
Farm laborer			*	*
Servant-cook			*	
Gardener			*	*
Physician			*	
Doctor			*	
Laborer on R.R.			*	
Miner			*	
Gambler			*	
Servant-keeps house			*	
Farmer			*	*
Servant-house work			*	
Running laundry			*	
Keeps wash house			*	
House cleaner				*
Doctor of medicine				*
Helper-fish market				*
Keep lodgers				*
Hop raiser				*

Morrow County (1885)

Male	1860	1870	1880	1900
Laundryman				*
Restaurant proprietor				*
Cook				*

Multnomah County (1854)

Female	1860	1870	1880	1900
Keeping house			*	
Laborer				*
Ironer				*
Servant				*
Prostitute				*
Male				

	Col 1	Col 2	Col 3
Washer & ironer *			
Washing	*	*	
Cook	*	*	*
Laundryman	*	*	*
Convict	*		*
Servant		*	*
Wash dishes		*	
Laborer		*	*
Collector		*	
Saws wood		*	
Merchant-dry goods		*	*
Merchant-tea			*
Tailor		*	
Pedlar		*	
Contractor		*	
Merchant		*	*
Jobbing		*	
Druggist		*	
Ironer		*	
Clerk in store		*	
Barber		*	*
Grubbing		*	
Farm laborer		*	*
Servant-cook		*	
Servant-keeps house		*	
Servant-house work		*	
Gardener		*	*
Physician		*	
Doctor		*	
Laborer on R.R.		*	
Laborer-rope works			*
Laborer-docks			*
Miner		*	

Gambler	*	
Farmer	*	*
Running laundry	*	
Keeps wash house	*	
House cleaner		*
Doctor of medicine		*
Helper-fish markets		*
Keep lodgers		*
Hop raiser		*
Canner		*
Fisherman		*
Lottery game		*
Tool sharpener		*
Junk gatherer		*
Porter		*
Labeler		*
Vegetable garden		*
Shoe maker		*
Waiter		*
Actor		*
Expressman		*
Teacher		*
Cigar dealer		*
Restaurant owner		*
Curio dealer		*

NOTE: from here down in the county list no data was gathered from the 1900 census.

Polk County (1845)

Male	1860	1870	1880
Cook		*	*
Mill Hand			*

Servant-cook	*
Servant	*
Laborer-R.R.	*
Laborer	*
Boss laborer	*
Wash house	*
Washing & ironing	*
Cook in hotel	*
Laundryman	*
Wood chopper	*
Works in pottery	*
Work in saw mill	*
Housework	*

Note: the were no Chinese listed in the 1860 census.

Umatilla County (1862)

Female	1860	1870	1880
Prostitute		*	*
Male			
Cook		*	*
Laundry		*	*
Gardener		*	
Washing		*	
Miner		*	
Wash house		*	*
Servant-cook			*
Laborer-R.R.			*
Cook-R.R.			*
Cook-hotel			*
Waiter			*
Domestic			*
Doctor			*

Union County (1864)

Female	1860	1870	1880
Prostitute			*
Keeping house		*	
Male			
Servant		*	*
Farm hand		*	*
Washerman		*	*
Cook		*	*
Miner		*	*
Wash house			*
Servant-cook			*
Herder			*
Merchant			*
Delivering goods			*
Collecting			*
Laborer			*
Clerk in store			*
Druggist & Doctor			*
Boarding house			*
Gambler			*
Ex-merchant			*
Gardener			*
Laundry			*
Shoe maker			*
Opium dealer			*
Tailor			*
Blacksmith			*
"Judge"			*

Wasco County (1854)

Female	1860	1870	1880
not reported	*		

	1860	1870	1880
Keeping house		*	*
Male			
Cook	*	*	*
Washerman	*		*
Domestic		*	*
Wood sawyer		*	*
Convict		*	
Physician		*	
Laundry		*	*
Hotel		*	
Washing & Ironing		*	
Cook-Steamboat		*	
Cook-Hotel			*
Works on R.R.			*
Book keeper			*
Washing			*
Clerk			*
Wash house			*
Keeping store			*
Doctor			*
Barber			*
Irons			*
Not reported			*
Gardener			*
Servant			*
Servant-Cook			*
Laborer			*

Washington County (1849)

Male	1860	1870	1880
Chair Mender			*
Cook			*
Contractor-Chinese			*

	1860	1870	1880
Laborer			*
Laborer-R.R.			*
Laundryman			*
Gardener			*
Wood chopper			*
Teamster			*
Not reported			*
Boss			*
Washerman			*
Farmer			*
Farm laborer			*

Note: no Chinese listed in 1860 or 1870 census.

Yamhill County (1843)

Male	1860	1870	1880
Domestic servant			*
Grubbing			*
Laundry			*
Servant			*
Servant-Cook			*
Section hand-R.R.			*
Laborer			*
Washing house			*
Prisoner			*
Washerman			*
Cook in hotel			*

Note: no Chinese reported in 1860 or 1870 census.

Chapter Six

Idaho

The first gold discovery, 30 September 1860, was in the Oro Fino - Pierce City district of north central Idaho with the towns of Oro Fino, Elk City, Newsome, Florence, Warren, and Pierce City, named after Captain E.D. Pierce, springing up between 1861-1862. Most of these gold mining towns lasted only as long as the gold boom (Trull 1946). Lewiston developed as a supply center for the mining activities. At its best, Elk City had eight stores, six saloons, three butcher shops, two blacksmith shops, and two express offices. For a time, Florence was Idaho's richest gold camp (Yu 1991).

A great influx of miners came from northern California. "The Mining Laws for the Oro Fino District" were adopted on 5 January 1861, within which it was stated that members of the Chinese and Asiatic races and South Pacific Ocean Islanders were to be excluded from the mining areas.

Between 1883 and 1884 another gold field was developed in the Coeur d'Alene district of northern Idaho with the usual restrictions to keep the Chinese from entering (Yu 1991).

In 1861 a prospector, Moses Splawn met a Bannock Indian while working in the northern Idaho area around Elk Creek and Florence and was told that he ought to look further south to find the "yellow sand" (Zhu 1997).

In 1862, two parties of men headed for the gold strikes in southern Idaho met at the confluence of the Snake and Boise

Rivers. They were George Grimes and a group from Auburn, Oregon, and Moses Splawn with another party from Florence, Idaho. They formed a single group and searched for gold in the basin and were attacked by the local Indians. Grimes died and the rest headed to the army depot at Walla Walla, Washington where they made a report. In the fall, a party headed back to Grimes Creek in the Boise Basin, the creek now named after the unfortunate Grimes, and staked claims. Zhu (1997) states that Splawn was from Auburn with six others and they met Grimes, a Portuguese emigrant recently arrived from Portland, with a group of eight others.

The Boise Basin, located 25 miles northeast of Boise, is a rather low basin, whose bottom is around 4,000 feet, surrounded by mountains, making it a rather isolated spot (Zhu 1997). Even before mining in the Basin could begin five mining camps had come into existence: Pioneerville and Centerville were built on Grimes Creek with Placerville established near Granite and Ophir creeks. Then at the junction of Mores and Elk creeks the beginnings of Bannock City occured in October 1862. Bannock City was renamed, becoming Idaho City on 20 February 1864, to keep it separate from Bannock, Montana in people's minds (Jones et al 1979; Yu 1991). The other mining camps were Boston and Hogem (Zhu 1997).

In excess of 2,500 mining claims were recorded in the Bannock City district, 2,000 in the Centerville district, and more than 4,500 in the Placerville district in July 1863 while the population in the basin hit 14,910. In 1864 the overall population dropped to 13,500 (Zhu 1997).

The Chinese entered the Boise Basin in 1864, perhaps as early as 1863 (Zhu 1997). By 1866-1867 there was 2,000 Chinese in the basin (Trull 1946).

The gold rush into Boise City, a mining town north of

Boise in southwestern Idaho, began in 1863 (the same year that the Washington and Idaho territories became separate entities). The bulk of the traffic traveled from Portland up the Columbia River to either Umatilla Landing or Wallula and then by road to Boise and points south or to Lewiston. A road was constructed between Sacramento and Boise, ca. 1865, with Chinese arriving in the Boise area about the same time (Jones et al 1979). Portland's newspaper complained loudly about being by-passed when the California Steam Navigation Company, headquartered in San Francisco, sought to open an "inside" route to southern Idaho via travel up the Sacramento River to Chico and then overland from there (Paul 1982). A road was constructed, in about 1865, by cutting through the northern passes of the Sierra Nevada Mountains into Susanville, to Summit Lake, then past Buffalo Springs, White Horse Meadow, and north to the Boise valley (Ling 1980).

Pack trains were first utilized to supply the various mines and as roads were constructed and built, freight wagons began to replace the pack trains. Chinese began to operate packs trains in 1862 (Trull 1946).

An exploring party in 1863 found gold in the Owyhee Mountains with the towns of Boonville, Ruby City, and Silver City rapidly being established with Chinese being noted as coming to Silver City in 1865 (Yu 1991). Placer mining started at Salomon and at Leesburg in 1866 (Trull 1946).

Eighty miles of ditch were constructed in 1863 to supply the necessary water to support placer mining around Mores Creek, near Idaho City.

Boise was established in 1864 at the same time that Fort Boise and the discovery of gold occured. Fort Boise was established to keep separate the indigenous population and the miners and emigrants. The town served as a supply center for gold mining in the Boise Basin and other areas (Jones 1980).

Wells Fargo and Company freighted goods between Boise and Idaho City (Ling 1980).

In 1865, in the Oro-Fino mining district, the Chinese were admitted due to the lack of laborers that were required to operate the mining activities. In the same year, A.W. Sweeney, a California clergyman, was invited to Lewiston to deliver a speech arguing that the Chinese had been devastating to California and to the interests of the American miners (Yu 1991).

Idaho City, by this time (1865), had a newspaper, two theaters, two photographic galleries, three express offices, four restaurants, four breweries, four drugstores, five groceries, six blacksmith shops, seven meat markets, seven bakeries, eight hotels, twelve doctors, twenty-two attorneys, twenty-four saloons, thirty-six general merchandise stores, along with other assorted businesses, and a population of 7,000 (Zhu 1997).

In 1866 a flume was constructed across Elk Creek for use at Buena Bar near Idaho City.

The Idaho Territorial Legislature issued a law, 24 December 1864, that Chinese miners had to pay $4.00 per month, raised on 11 January 1866, to $5.00. The tax collectors were allowed to keep 20% of the money collected (Yu 1991).

The population in Idaho in 1870 was around 18,000 of which there were 5,600 Indians, 4,272 Chinese, and 68 black people. But by this time most of the early placer claims had declined causing a general economic recession throughout the mining areas of the state. Supply towns, like Lewiston experienced severe economic declines as a result (Yu 1991). Zhu (1997) states that the Ninth U.S. Census gives 14,999 residents for Idaho in 1870, but almost the same number, 4,274, of Chinese. Inside the Boise Basin however the Chinese were 49.3% of the total population, 1,740 out of a total 3,528 residents and had become the dominant labor force in the mining activities there. Ling (1980) lists the total miner population in Idaho in 1870 as 6,579, with 3,853 being Chinese.

The Boise Basin, unlike many others areas in the west, remained a gold mining region for almost a century shifting from placer to lode mining over time (Zhu 1997).

Anti-Chinese antagonism increased in the 1870s as Chinese laborers entered economic areas other than mining. In 1886, the first anti-Chinese convention was held in Boise.

The *Idaho Tri-Weekly Statesman*, 22 April, 1876 stated: "The Chinese who came to this country are of the very lowest grade, extremely ignorant . . . they are filthy and strictly dishonest, utterly destitute of any moral sense or consciousness" (Ling 1980). Discrimination became official when Idaho became a state in 1890, essentially following the behaviors of the other western states (Yu 1991).

Chapter Seven

Closing The Gate

With the exception of a few years after they entered the United States, the Chinese were a target of various forms of harassment and violence. Much of this stemmed from the cultural views of the times that only the Europeans were important and all other races were somehow inferior and that treating these others as such was not something to worry about or to be bothered by.

The Anglo-American racism resulting from slavery began to develop in California about the time of the Annexation of California to the United States in 1846. The feeling that minority groups were a fearful competition in the labor market and that it would be "degrading" for those forced to work alongside the Negro, the Oriental, or the Indian, grew rapidly in the ensuring years (Heizer and Almquist 1971).

There had already been anti-foreign and color prejudice but it was intensified by the presence of American Southerners, about one-third of the early population in California during these times (Dicker 1979). The terminology and racial qualities previously assigned to blacks were transferred to the Chinese Takaki 1979).

As we have seen, harassment and violence began during the earliest days of the gold mining era in the west in California and expanded rapidly into a wide-spread series of ever accumulating nonsense that eventually led up to the exclusion acts passed by the Congress of the United States. The rabble rousing attracted, as it always seems to do, those politicians who felt pandering to this behavior was good for their political careers. The Republicans as well as other politicians found it politically expedient to be nominally anti-Chinese as they curried favor with the laboring classes (Clyde and Bears 1966).

In 1852, Hinton Helper, soon the chief Republican spokesman against slavery stated "No inferior race of men can exist in these United States without becoming subordinate to the will of the Anglo-Americans . . . It is so with the Negroes in the South; it is so with the Irish in the North; it is so with the Indians in New England; and it will be so with the Chinese in California" (Saxton 1995).

One of the earliest of the rabble rousers was Denis Kearney, born in Oakmont, County Cork, Ireland, 1 February 1857, who settled in San Francisco in 1868. In 1877, he began agitating this fellow workmen mostly against the rights of capital and the importation of Chinese Labor. Eventually he formed and dominated The Workingmen's Party which met every Sunday afternoon on a vacant property, called a sandlot, hence the nicknames of the group, "sandlotters," and "Sandlot Party" (Dicker 1979). With the encouragement of the mayor of San Francisco, I.S. Kalloch, Kearney denounced the Chinese for "working hand-in-hand with monopolies, of accepting slave wages and of robbing the white man of his job." He stated "I made up my mind that if our civilization – California civilization – was to continue, Chinese immigration must be stopped . . . " (Bryce 1889; Nokes 2009; Currier 1928). However, Kearney stated in 1877: "I am opposed to strikes in the Republic, where the ballot of a millionaire's gardener or coachman cancels that of their master" (Bryce 1889). Kearney traveled to the eastern part of the United States to win further support for his anti-Chinese views but soon faded into obscurity (Hicks 1937; Dicker 1979).

Sowell (1996) pointed out that the political charges thrown about were based on the false assumption that "there is either a fixed or preordained level of wealth" that can be had and that the Chinese, by sending funds back home were damaging to other wage earners and their ability to gain wealth. In actually, the sums taken by the Chinese were:

1) a fraction of the wealth they created [by their endeavors] and added to the host country's economy;

2) that what the Chinese spend in-country, wherever they were located, had little effect on the local non-Chinese in terms of the money sent overseas, that is, the money they kept for themselves had no bearing on anyone else's well-being. None-the-less, these political charges were politically effective regardless of their bogus nature.

Prior to this, as the easy rich surface claims of the gold fields in California became exhausted, the Chinese were accused by the white miners of stealing the miners wealth. They asserted that California's gold belonged only to them. And the battle cry from them was, "California for the Americans."

The Governor of California, Bigler, jumped on the band wagon and sent a message to the California legislature wherein he stated that the Chinese were "avaricious, ignorant of moral obligations, incapable of being assimilated, and dangerous to the public welfare."

The yield in the California placers declined in 1853-1854. This coupled with the discovery of gold in Australia brought on the financial panic of 1854. The labor market was glutted with people seeking employment. It was proclaimed widely that the Chinese tended to injure the interests of the working class and degrade labor, that is, they deprived white men of positions by taking lower wage jobs and that they were leaches sucking the very life-blood from the country because they sent a portion of their wages back to China. The American labor of which so much was made was mainly composed of the Irish and other Europeans who were, in fact, no more American than the Chinese that they were against. However, they could vote while the Chinese could not (Norton 1924).

An article in the Shasta Republican, 18 December 1856, cited in Dicker (1979) stated:

> Hundreds of Chinamen have been slaughtered in cold blood in the last five years by the desperadoes that infest the state, The murder of Chinamen was almost a daily occurrence, yet in all this time we have heard of but two or three cases where guilty parties were brought to justice . . . Many persons have avowed themselves opposed to the execution of white men for the murder of Chinamen.

Portland, Oregon, saw greater mob violence in 1866. Forty Chinese who worked at the Oregon City Woolen Mills were forced from their homes by a mob of about sixty. That evening a mob of 7-8 hundred anti-Chinese demonstrators paraded through Portland complete with a brass band. The next month (March) fifty masked men drove 100-200 Chinese laborers from Mt. Tabor and Albina. Thirty armed whites, masked or with blackened faces, attacked Chinese gardeners in Guilds Lake while burning a few homes.

On 18 October 1871, nineteen Chinese were murdered and seventeen lynched in Los Angeles although Chen (1972) gives the number as twenty-one with fifteen hanged on the spot. Pfaelzer (2008) states that seventeen Chinese were lynched and two knifed to death. Buildings were looted (of over $40,000) and burned. The police mostly stood and watched, in some cases aided and abetted the mob. While a grand jury indicted somewhere between 30 to 150 men only six, or eight, were sentenced to short jail terms (Norton 1924), two to six years (Pfaelzer 2008). Three weeks later all were released (Pfaelzer 2008).

In 1872, it was reported in Baker City, Oregon, that two whites had smashed windows in the Chinese settlement there (Edson 1974).

The panic of 1873 merely added to the turmoil and it increased even more when the western business world essentially crashed in 1877 (Norton 1924). Tens of thousands of both Chinese and Caucasian workers were laid off with workers turning to violent competition for scare jobs.

On June 18, 1873, the Oregon Anti-Chinese Association was organized in Portland (F.R. Naile, Chairman). Its members were pledged to: discourage Chinese immigration; never to employ Chinese workers; try to prevent other employers from hiring Chinese workers; and, to refuse to vote for any candidate that would not pledge himself to serve the principles of the association. A branch was organized in Oregon City, July 15, 1873 (Chen, C. 1972)

California, in 1876, felt the full impact of the current depression coupled with a great drought. By 1877 from one-fifth to one-quarter of the available white labor force was unemployed. Both major political parties, Republican and Democrat, had in 1876 adopted anti-Chinese planks in their national platforms in order to get the vote of the labor factions in the west, such as the Workingman's Party (Saxton 1995; Hong 1925).

In Idaho, at Orogrande near Loon Creek, February 1879, nineteen Chinese miners were attacked by white men dressed as Indians, thirteen died and six escaped. For years the "Sheepherder" Indians were blamed (Yu 1991).

California workingmen calling themselves the Order of Caucasians would undertake the systematic killing of the

Chinese in order to preserve other workingmen from total ruin due to lack of jobs at an economic level they felt they deserved. The labor force in the state shared a conviction of displacement and deprivation in the labor market by the Chinese being hired, that is, competitors for jobs (Saxton 1995).

1880-1890 was the decade when the anti-Chinese agitation rose to its most extreme level. President Rutherford B. Hayes, in 1879, suggested, as Congress began to pass laws that were anti-Chinese in nature, "We shall oppress the Chinaman, and their presence will make hoodlums and vagabonds of their oppressors" (Steiner 1979).

A new treaty was signed in 1880 which gave the United States the right to "regulate, limit, or suspend" immigration of Chinese laborers, thus limiting the more open-ended Burlingame Treaty. From all accords it appears this was a direct result of pressure mainly from the West Coast. Only teachers, students, merchants, and tourists were allowed entry (Hong 1925). Congress attempted to totally suspend the immigration of Chinese labor for twenty years but the president vetoed the move.

Congress passed a series of acts targeting the Chinese population.

The Act of May 6th, 1882 (22 Stat. 58), signed by President Chester A. Arthur, 8 May 1882, suspended immigration of Chinese laborers, defined as both skilled and unskilled laborers and Chinese employed in mining, for ten years; permitted Chinese who had been resident in the United States as of 17 November 1880 to obtain certificates from the Collector of Customs which entitled the Chinese to return to the United States after a temporary absence; admitted Chinese persons other than laborers upon the production of a certificate from the Chinese government, in English, describing the immigrant and certifying his right to come to the United States under terms of the treaty. Between 1882 and 1885 Chinese immigrants into the United States dropped from 39,579 to 22 (LaLande 1981).

This document became known as the "Section Six Certificate." The act also provided for the deportation of Chinese persons who had entered the United States temporarily after the passage of the act upon the order of a judge or commissioner of a Court of the United States. The act also stated "That hereafter no State court or court of the U.S. shall admit Chinese to citizenship."

The act was amended by the Act of 5 July 1884 (23 Stat. 115) which stated that the Section Six Certificate now required an antecedent visa from the place of departure by the American Counsel who had to verify the facts provided in the certificate. It also stated that the law applied to ethnic Chinese regardless of their country of origin.

The Act of 1882 stimulated other countries to do the same thing: New Zealand, restriction, 1881, exclusion 1920; Canada, restriction 1885, exclusion 1923; Natal, exclusion 1897; Orange Free State, exclusion 1899; Australia, exclusion 1901; Cape of Good Hope, exclusion 1904; and, Transvaal, exclusion 1907 (Lai & Choy 1971).

Portland Mayor John Gates with the backing of the Editor, Harvey Scott, of *The Oregonian* newspaper, organized a force of about one thousand to provide security for the Chinese in the city. He also organized most of the city leaders to join with him. This ended the Chinese agitation in Portland (Nokes 2009).

In 1885, during the months of September and October, the anti-Chinese associations met in Portland, Tacoma, and Seattle. Endless meetings were held in Portland calling for Chinese expulsion, but little action was taken. The *Oregonian* was boycotted for opposing the movement and for stating the obvious reasons for doing so. The *Oregonian* was the leading newspaper in Oregon. During the 45 year leadership of Harvey W. Scott (1865-1910), it had come down strongly on the side of law-and-order. A typical editorial illustrates Scott's treatment and attitude toward the disorders being urged by the anti-Chinese movements.

> Within a radius of ten miles of Portland thousand of acres of heavy forest have been cleared away by Chinese labor; the stumps have been removed and the land brought into a fine state of cultivation. Hundreds of white persons around us are finding employment and support for themselves and families in the cultivation and further improvement of these lands. The labor of the Chinese has been the basis of it all . . .
>
> This work is of a kind which white men will not pursue for any length of time . . . Contracts let to white men for clearing land have usually been abandoned by them. . . They boast of their irresponsibility, and take pleasure in causing their employer disappointment and loss . . . Farmers and others, unable to get white labor that would fulfill its engagements, have turned to the Chinese, who at least show fidelity in this regard. But it is this very quality that makes the Chinese so hated by the irresponsible white who rally at the call of agitators and pretended champions of labor . . .
>
> On the whole, then, the Chinese do not deprive white persons of employment. If they do, in some cases, they plainly make more employment for white persons in others. The employment of white upon the thousands of acres of land open to cultivation through Chinese labor, prove this; so likewise does the employment of white in

large numbers, in connection with the great fish packing industry, which, without Chinese labor as auxiliary or foundation, never would have been developed, and could not go on.

What is needed most of all in this country is the utterance of sense on this subject, as a foil or check to the floods of injurious nonsense with which it is deluged . . . (quoted in Chen, C. 1972).

David Newsom in an article published in *The Pacific Christian Advocate*, 12 October 1876 (Newsom 1972) discussed much the same thing.

There are hundreds of thousands of acres of the very best arable lands in Western Oregon that remain *untilled*. Why is this so? The reason is, that those land are more or less set in brush. At the rates charged heretofore by our men for grubbing out and preparing these lands for the plow, the owners could not afford it. And not more than one man in every ten who pass around hunting for work, will not look a mattock or blade square in the face.

*   *   *   *   *

Chinamen are scattering out all over Western Oregon grubbing and clearing up the brush lands for the plow, at one-half the rates charged by the white – Chinese board themselves in all cases (emphasis in original article).

The floor of the Willamette Valley in Oregon was mostly prairie when the first settlers arrived, the result of the continuous burning by the indigenous population, the Indians. After the settlers drove out the Indians those prairie areas not immediately cultivated began to revert to brush and small trees. By 1800, the lands, known as "grub lands," were being cleared for cultivation. This clearing process was thus called "grubbing." In a letter to the *Oregonian*, July 28, 1880, it was stated:

> The Chinese have been paid about ten dollars per acre for grubbing and 85 cents per cord for cutting the grubs into cord wood. The farmers have generally burnt the limbs and roots.

Mobs in San Francisco set fire to Chinatown and murdered thirteen Chinese over a three month period in 1885. In the same year, a white mob encouraged by Mayor Jacon Weisbach, a German immigrant, evicted three hundred, some report two hundred, Chinese from Tacoma, Washington Territory, and dumped them in a forest far from town in the winter while their homes and business were looted and burned. The police stood and watched. The mayor and the sheriff hid at city hall while the mobs ran unchecked. Governor Squire ignored telegrams from Chinese urging him to intervene (Knoll 1982; Pfaelzer 2008). Some of these evicted folk would move down to Portland. There then followed the forced removal of the Chinese in Washington from Pierce, King, Kitsap, Snohomish, Skagit, and Whitcom counties from a number of the smaller towns including Port Townsend and Bellingham Bay (Willson and MacDonald 1983). Finally, at the urging of Washington Governor Watson Squire, apparently now alarmed at the spreading violence that he had chosen to ignore earlier, President Cleveland dispatched troops from Fort Vancouver to quell white mobs in Seattle (Chen 1972).

In the years from 1850 to 1905, in the several states, there were nearly 200 hundred of these events as the Chinese were systematically driven from their homes (Pfaelzer 2008).

On 2 September 1885, a mob of white miners attacked and killed twenty-eight with fifteen wounded, some report forty-two, coal miners working for the Union Pacific Railroad at Rock Springs, Wyoming Territory and burned the entire village of seventy-nine Chinese houses with property destroyed at a value of $150,000 (Saxton 1995). Swartout (1982) gives figures of twenty-eight Chinese dead and fifteen wounded. The railroad had employed 300 Chinese and about 150 whites to work the coal mine there. Saxton (1995) gives the figures of 331 Chinese, 150 whites. Chinese men and women were killed and their bodies thrown into the burning structures (Chen, C. 1972). Up until 1875 the mines had been worked only by white miners, but during a labor dispute the company brought in Chinese workers with the eventual attacks prompted by the feeling among the white workers that their favored position in the labor force was being reduced (Saxton 1995).

One of the most often quoted anti-Chinese events was the massacre of a party of Chinese miners on the Snake River in Oregon. An article cited by Tucker (1981) gives the date of the event as being on or about May 25, 1887, with the number of Chinese being thirty-one, implicating seven white men. Another account states ten Chinese in 1888 (Jasper 1971). Chen, C. (1972) gives thirty-one Chinese and five white men in 1887, while Edson (1974) says seven white men killed ten Chinese in June 1887. The Chinese Minister Chang Yen Hoon protested the incident to Secretary of State Bayard and the United States paid $276,610.75 indemnities to the Imperial Chinese government in order to forestall an international incident (Tucker 1981).

The mass killing of Chinese miners began on 25 May 1887 while they were working on Deep Creek on the Snake River in Hells Canyon, Oregon (see Nokes 2009 for a much more detailed discussion of the event than the following paragraphs present).

Hells Canyon, at its widest, is roughly ten miles wide having an average depth of 5,500 feet with the deepest section, measured from rim to rim, is 7,913 feet. The Grande Canyon by comparison is 6,100 feet deep. Running through the canyon is the Snake river, the thirteenth longest river in North America, originating in Yellowstone National Park. Hells Canyon is about ninety miles long.

The gang, mostly small time rustlers, responsible for this carnage were all residents of Wallowa County, northeastern Oregon. A few were tried for murder but all were declared innocent mainly through the actions of friends and family. One would eventually move to Idaho and live a prosperous life. All-in-all, it appears the event was the subject of a massive coverup that lasted more than one hundred years, a coverup that includes hiding the records of the trial by county clerks and so-called "histories" of Wallowa County written by local folk that make no mention of the event at all.

Bruce "Blue" Evans, thirty-one at the time, was the leader of the gang. He was a small-time rancher, and like the others of his gangs, more interested in making money quickly with the least amount of labor being expended. The gang members were: J. Titus Canfield, age 21, Evan's chief sidekick; Hezekiah "Carl" Hughes, age 37; Hiram Maynard, age 38; Omar LaRue, late teens, early twenties; Robert McMillan, age 15; and, Frank Vaughan, age 21-22, who then turned against the others during the trail.

The investigation into the incident began when a body was found floating near Lime Kiln, thirty miles south of Lewiston in the Snake River. Within days six more bodies were found. The final estimate of dead was given as thirty-six, but the exact number has never been determined. Bodies were found with gunshots wounds in the back as well as brutalized by axe wounds.

Judge Joseph K. Vincent, justice of the peace for Nez Perce County, which includes Lewiston, and a U.S. Commissioner, stated: "It was the most cold-blooded cowardly treachery, I have ever heard tell of on this coast. And I am a 49er. Every one was shot, cut up and stripped and thrown into the river."

There was, by and large, a great lack of interest in investigating the incident, a reflection of the attitudes toward the Chinese at the time. Oregon's Governor at the time, Sylvestor Pennoyer, elected in 1877, after chairing an assembly of around one thousand agitators demanding the removal of the Chinese from Portland, was one of the leaders of the anti-Chinese crusade in Portland.

It wasn't until nine months after the incident in 1888 that the Chinese legation in Washington, D.C. informed the Secretary of State, Thomas F. Bayard, who was said to believe that unrestrained immigration from China threatened white control of the American West.

Before the trial thirty-four prominent country residents, all men, all property owners, filed an appeal to the Circuit Court to set bail to free Hughes, Maynard, and McMillam, as these upstanding citizens claimed the three were being "illegally held," even though a grand jury had returned an indictment. Circuit Judge Luther Isom approved releasing them on bail stating that the evidence against them appeared weak.

Evans escaped from the county jail at gunpoint after subduing a deputy sheriff and was for the rest of his life a fugitive. Canfield, and La Rue fled the county. Evans and Canfield were also wanted on rustling charges.

Most of the anti-Chinese violence was concentrated on the west side of the Cascades in Oregon although not altogether. In 1885 (February 12) a fire broke out in the

Chinese portion of Canyon City. When the fire was over the Chinese were not allowed to rebuild and were urged to go elsewhere. The bulk of them resettled in the Chinese section of John Day (Chen, C. 1972).

Mass demonstrations in the mid-1880s occurred widely in California: Santa Barbara, Pasadena, Santa Ana, Santa Cruz, Healdsburg, Red Bluff, Merced, Placerville, Los Angeles, Sacramento, Yuba City, Reding, Petaluma, Vallejo, Chico, Nevada City, and Oakland. Humbolt and Del Norte counties evicted all resident Chinese to outside their borders. It was during this period that the term "yellow peril" was coined. The California Legislature in 1882 declared a legal holiday to encourage public demonstrations against the admission of Chinese to the United States (Heizer and Almquist 1971).

The 13 February 1886 issue of the *Boise City Republican* carried an article of the anti-Chinese Convention in Portland, Oregon, urging the same thing in Idaho. The Idaho territorial delegation set it up and the Idaho Anti-Chinese Convention was held on 25 February 1886. Most of the small town newspapers jumped on the bandwagon (Yu 1991). However, in Idaho, the Anti-Chinese League failed to force out all the Chinese. This then became a big political issue in the state in the fall of 1886 with each political party accusing the other of being a "Chinese-lover" with each party sticking an anti-Chinese plank into the party platform in order to woo the voters (Trull 1946).

The Act of 13 September 1888 (25 Stat. 476) stated that a Chinese laborer who had departed from the United States was not permitted to return unless he had a lawful wife, child, or parent in the United States, or property valued at $1,000. And even fulfilling these conditions, the return certificate was only valid for one year, the length could be extended in certain contingencies. The act was introduced by William Scott of Pennsylvania, chair of the Democratic National Campaign Committee, and passed the House unanimously with slight resistence in the Senate. It was upheld by the Supreme Court.

As the bulk of Chinese laborers were males who either were unmarried or did not bring their wives with them, this act effectively barred most of the Chinese population currently in the United States from returning if they left.

The Act of 1 October 1888 (25 Stat. 505). known as the Scott Act, prohibited the return of any Chinese laborer who departed from the United States, and forbid the issuance of return certificates to Chinese laborers resident in the United States. The act also cancelled outstanding return certificate already issued to Chinese laborers who had left the country on temporary visits abroad.

Fiftieth Congress, Session 1, CHAP. 1064. An act a supplement to an act entitled "An act to execute certain treaty stipulations relating to Chinese," approved the sixth day of May eighteen hundred and eighty-two.

Be it enacted by the Senate and House of Representatives of the United States of America in Congress assembled, That from and after the passage of this act, it shall be unlawful for any Chinese laborer who shall at any time heretofore have been, or who may now or hereafter be, a resident within the United States, and who shall have departed, or shall depart, therefrom, and shall not have returned before the passage of this act, to return to, or remain in, the United States.

SEC. 2. That no certificates of identity provided for in the fourth and fifth sections of the act to which this is a supplement shall hereafter be issued; and every certificate heretofore issued in pursuance thereof is hereby declared void and of no effect, and the chinese laborer claiming admission by virtue thereof shall not be permitted to enter the United States.

SEC. 3. That all the duties prescribed, liabilities penalties and forfeitures imposed, and the powers conferred by the second, tenth, eleventh, and twelfth, sections of the act to which this is a supplement are hereby extended and made applicable to the provisions of this act.

SEC. 4. That all such part or parts of the act to which this is a supplement as are inconsistent herewith are hereby repealed.

These acts stopped the re-entry of approximately 20,000 Chinese laborers.

In the decade of 1890-1990 Congress continued to pass acts that were ever more restricting against the Chinese.

The Act of 5 May 1892 (27 Stat. 25), known as the Geary Act, extended all the Chinese exclusion laws for a period of ten years; placed the burden of establishing their lawful right to remain in the United States on the Chinese involved in the deportation proceedings; required registration, within one year, of all Chinese laborers in the United States; and provided for the issuance of Certificates of Residence; and stated that any found without such a certificate were subject to deportation.

In 1893, the 53rd Congress decided that there were an estimated 85,000 Chinese living in the United States that had not registered under the Geary Act (12,243 Chinese had registered). Those not registered should be tried and deported. The Secretary of State asked for the estimate of the cost to do the job. It was estimated to cost in excess of 10 million dollars. Congress repealed, on November 3, 1893, the requirement to execute the deportation proceedings (Heizer and Almquist 1971).

The Act of 3 November 1893 (28 Stat. 7), known as the McCreary amendment, extended the time for registration for the Chinese laborers by six months; defined "laborer" and "merchant"; and, prohibited the release on bail of Chinese persons under order of deportation.

The Act of 7 July 1898 (30 Stat. 750) prohibited further immigration of Chinese into the Hawaiian Islands except under conditions that were similar to the continental United States.

Heizer and Almquist (1971) argue forcefully that "history tells us that no more sorry record exists in the Union [of the United States] of inhuman and uncivil treatment toward minority groups than in California. . . in American history – in the shoddy excuses used for seizing California from Mexico, the ignoring of the plainly worded provisions in the Treaty of Guadalupe Hildago of 1848 guaranteeing the rights of pre-1848 residents, and in the cruel discrimination against Indians, Mexicans, Japanese, Chinese, Negroes, and Filipinos – there is no record to equal that of the people of the Golden State."

If this seems harsh, Pfaelzer (2008) documents in detail the ethnic cleansing of the Chinese from more than 200 communities, as well as murders and mass lootings, stimulated by the widespread hysteria created by labor unions, politicians, newspapers, the wealthy and the poor, that ran rampant across California and towns of neighboring states for over fifty years. Essentially, the Chinese functioned as a universal scapegoat for any ill, real or imagined, that could be abused, beaten, robbed, murdered, or run out of town without fear. In almost no case were the non-Chinese ever brought before the law with anything happening that mattered, or if a few were, nothing happened to them.

A question rarely asked, but hinted at, here and there in the literature, is: what kind of cultural, and cultural values, gave rise to such atrocious behavior? It was not just some lonely bigot here or there, it was a wide spread phenomenon that repeated some of the worse nonsense in town after town, camp after camp throughout California and propagated itself outwards.

Anon (1925) stated that in 1855 there were 489 murders in the state of California and only six legal executions which gives a hint of some major problem in the culture of the time. Heizer and Almquist (1971), as did Pfaelzer (2008), demonstrated a history of deliberate extermination of the Indians as well as massive discrimination of any other group deemed not-white. Pfaelzer (2008) lists all the greed behind the elimination of the Indians as a means to take their lands and resources.

We have noted the importation of the negative racial values coming into the state from the deep South.

Perhaps it was nothing more than a culture of greed coupled with a self-centered sense of privilege that started with the taking of the land from Mexico which then grew into a virulent strain of institutional insanity?

In California there developed a conviction among the white population of racial superiority with the first victims being those from lands south of the American border, then indigenous Indians, but in the main the Chinese (Saxton 1995). Saxton suggests that there was a coupling of the political goals of the major political parties and the values expressed during the beginnings of the labor unions which often viewed the Chinese as tools of monopolies. This belief system created the great separation between these groups and the Chinese. A strong anti-Chinese crusade became a powerful organizing tool.

This behavior as mentioned in the above few paragraphs was what has been defined as a "moral panic" (Goode and Ben-Yehuda 1994).

In a moral panic there tends to be a strong and widespread fear, or concern, that evil doing are happening, that there are certain enemies of society that are trying to bring harm to some of the people, or even to all of the people. This fear, or concern, tends to be out of proportion to the threat that seems to be posed by the behavior, or supposed behavior, of those responsible for that threat. Stemming from this perception is the sense of crisis and resultant feeling that something must be done without which the presumed suffering will be even greater.

In a moral panic, a group or a category of behavior is thought to be engaged in unacceptable, or immoral, behavior which is the cause, or is responsible, for the assumed serious harmful behavior. This then, is seen as a threat to their well-being, their basic values, and the interests of the society assumed to be threatened. The assumed perpetrators come to be regarded as the enemy of society, as deviants, outsiders, and thus legitimate and deserving targets of self-righteous anger, hostility, and punishment.

Zhu (1997), however, points out that the Chinese in the Boise Basin, Idaho, had a rather better time of it in terms of material comforts, economic mobility, justice, and social equality. A rare occurrence, indeed.

A final word from David Newsom in an article published in *The Pacific Christian Advocate*, 2 January 1879 (Newsom 1972) which seems as appropriate today as it was then.

> It is frequently the case that men find it easier
> to drift upon the tide of public opinion – be
> that opinion ever so erroneous – than to stand
> squarely and advocate the right, though in a
> lean minority. Men's passions often misguide
> them, and they run into grievous errors. And,

in most cases, public furors are brought about by a few men who exercise a controlling influence upon the masses. Very few do not stop to reason upon questions of the moment to the public, but jump at the conclusions of leading men.

*   *   *   *   **

It is a common accepted dogma, that the voice of the majority should be conclusive in all events. This seems to be true Republican Democratic doctrine. But there is another code in morals yet higher than the impulse of the masses: "Thou shall not follow a multitude to do *evil*."

*   *   *   *   **

The mere fact that any political party is in power does not conclusively prove that all their acts are just and equitable. Sober, well-informed, honest minorities have often preserved in their efforts for the right; and when the masses come to their sober reason, they came over to the minority, and when united, they became the majority (emphasis in original).

Citations

Anon

    1848   "The Excitement and enthusiasm of Gold Washing still continues – increases." *California Star* (Saturday, June 10, 1857).

    1925   *San Francisco News Letter*, The Jubilee Edition.

    1938   Prospectus. Camp Carson Gold Placer. Union County, Oregon.

Barlow, Jeffrey, and Christine Richardson

    1979   CHINA DOCTOR OF JOHN DAY. Portland, Oregon: Binford & Mort.

Barklow, Irene

    1987   FROM TRAILS TO RAILS: THE POST OFFICES, STAGE STOPS & WAGON ROADS OF UNION COUNTY, OREGON. Enterprise, Oregon: Enchantments Publishing of Oregon.

Barth, Gunther

    1964   BITTER STRENGTH: A HISTORY OF THE CHINESE IN THE UNITED STATES, 1850-1870. Cambridge: Harvard University Press.

Baxter, Farel R.

    1977   BYGONE SETTLEMENTS AND OUTPOSTS OF NORTHEASTERN

OREGON. Writer's Project Series, Number
6. Association of Oregon Geographers.

Bedrock Democrat - Baker City, OR
24 October 1871.
9 December 1895.
17 April 1872
5 April 1873

Beebe, Lucius, and Clegg, Charles
1949   U.S. WEST: THE SAGA OF WELLS
FARGO. E. P. Dutton & Co., Inc.: New
York.

Beeching, Jack
1975   THE CHINESE OPIUM WARS. New York:
Harcourt Brace Jovanovich.

Blair, Mrs. Philip
1927   Letter to L.M. Duncan. On file, La Grande
Ranger District.

Bolino, August C.
1958   "The Role of Mining in the Economic
Development of Idaho Territory." *Oregon
Historical Quarterly*(June), LIX (2), pp:
116-151.

Bright, Verne
1961   "Blue Mountain Eldorado: Auburn 1861."
Oregon Historic Quarterly, Vol. LXII
(September 1961), pp. 213-236.

Bryce, Viscount James
1889   THE AMERICAN COMMONWEALTH, Vol. II, second edition, revised. New York: MacMillan and Co.

Chen, Chia-Lin
1972   A Gold Dream in the Blue Mountains: A Study of the Chinese Immigrants in the John Day Area, Oregon, 1870-1910. Unpublished Masters Thesis - History, Portland State University, Portland, Oregon.

Chen, Jack
1980   THE CHINESE OF AMERICA. San Francisco: Harper & Row.

Cheng, Yu-Kwei
1956   FOREIGN TRADE AND INDUSTRIAL DEVELOPMENT OF CHINA: AN HISTORICAL AND INTEGRATED ANALYSIS THROUGH 1948. Washington, D.C.: University Press of Washington, D. C.

Chiu, Ping
1967   CHINESE LABOR IN CALIFORNIA, 1850-1880: AN ECONOMIC STUDY. The State Historic Society of Wisconsin for the Department of History, University of Wisconsin, Madison, Wisconsin.

Chu, Wen-Djang
> 1949 The Background of The Chinese Immigration Into The United States. Master of Arts thesis. University of Washington.

Chu, Daniel, and Samuel Chu
> 1967 PASSAGE TO THE GOLDEN GATE: A HISTORY OF THE CHINESE IN AMERICA TO 1910. New York: Doubleday & Company, Inc.

Clark, Malcolm, Jr.
> 1974 "The Bigot Disclosed: 90 Years of Nativism." *Oregon Historical Quarterly*, Vol. LXXV (June 1974), pp. 109-187.

Clyde, Paul H., and Burton F. Beers
> 1966 THE FAR EAST. A HISTORY OF THE WESTERN IMPACT AND THE EASTERN RESPONSE (1830-1965). Englewood Cliffs, New Jersey: Prentice-Hall, Inc.

Conwell, Russell H.
> 1871 WHY AND HOW: WHY THE CHINESE EMIGRATE, AND THE MEANS THEY ADOPT FOR THE PURPOSE OF REACHING AMERICA. Boston, Mass: Lee and Shepard.

Coolidge, Mary R.
> 1909 "Chinese Labor Competition On the Pacific Coast." *American Academy Of Political and*

Social Science Annuals, Vol. XXXIV.

Corbett, P. Scott, and Nancy Parker Corbett
1978   "The Chinese in Oregon, c. 1870-1880."
        Oregon Historical Quarterly (March), Vol.
        LXXVIII, No. 1.

Currier, Viola Noon
1928   The Chinese Web in Oregon History. M.A.
        Thesis. University of Oregon.

Davis, Rebecca
1960   "Great Gold Rush Brought Pioneers to
        Union County." In, *Supplement to History of
        Union County*, No.4, pp. 18-22. La Grande,
        OR.: Union County Historical Society.

DeFault, David
1959   "Chinese in the Mining Camps of
        California: 1848-1870." *Historical Society of
        Southern California Quarterly*, (June), pp.
        155-170.

Dicken, Samuel N., and Emily F. Dicken
1979   TWO CENTURIES OF OREGON
        GEOGRAPHY: VOL. I - THE MAKING OF
        OREGON, A STUDY IN HISTORICAL
        GEOGRAPHY. Oregon Historical Society:
        Portland, Oregon.

Dicker, Lavern Mau
1979   THE CHINESE IN SAN FRANCISCO: A
        PICTORIAL HISTORY. New York: Dover

Publications, Inc.

Doxiadis, C. A.
    1970 "Ekistics, the Science of Human Settlements." *Science,* Vol. 170, No. 3956, pp. 393-403.

DuFault, David V.
    1959 "The Chinese in the Mining Camps of California: 1848-1870." *Historical Society of California,* Quarterly, June.

Duncan, Ray, Sr.
    1970 The Big Ditch: A Story of Goldmining Days in Malheur County, Oregon. Unpublished paper. Eastern Oregon University.

Eastern Oregon News, Baker, Oregon
    31 March 1939.

Eastern Oregon Observer, La Grande
    27 July 1900.

Edson, Christopher Howard
    1974 THE CHINESE IN EASTERN OREGON, 1860-1890. San Francisco: R & E Research Associates.

EOO (Eastern Oregon Observer, La Grande, Oregon)
    1898a April 28
    1898b May 5

Evening Observer, La Grande, Oregon
    30 March 1939

Feuchtwang, Stephan D. R.
    1974   AN ANTHROPOLOGICAL ANALYSIS
           OF CHINESE GEOMANCY. Vithagna.

Freedman, Maurice
    1966   "Chinese Lineage and Society: Fukien and
           Kwangtung." *London School of Economics,
           Monographs On Social Anthropology*, No. 33.
           Humanities Press: New York.

Friday, Chris
    1982   Silent Sojourn: The Chinese Along the
           Lower Columbia River, 1870-1900.
           Unpublished History Honors Thesis,
           Lewis and Clark College, Portland,
           Oregon.

Gehr, Elliott; John R. Nelson, and Roger A. Walke
    1978   Cultural Resources Overview: Ironside EIS
           Area. Pro-Lysts, Inc. Eugene, Oregon.

Gernet, Jacques
    1982   A   HISTORY   OF CHINESE
           CIVILIZATION. New York: Cambridge
           University Press.

Goode, Erich and Nachman Ben-Yehuda
    1994   MORAL   PANICS.   THE   SOCIAL
           CONSTRUCTION   OF   DEVIANCE.

Malden MA: Blackwell Publishers, Inc.

Grande Ronde Sentinel, La Grande, Oregon
2 May 1868.

Griffen, Eldon
1938   CLIPPERS AND CONSULS: AMERICAN
CONSULAR AND COMMERCIAL
RELATIONS WITH EASTERN ASIA,
1845-1860. Wilmington, Delaware:
Scholarly Resources, Inc. (Reprint in 1972
of 1938 edition).

Hanes III, W. Travis and Frank Sanello
2002   THE OPIUM WARS. THE ADDICTION
OF ONE EMPIRE AND THE
CORRUPTION OF ANOTHER.
Naperville, Illinois: Sourcebooks, Inc.

Hayes, James
1980   "Chinese Clan Genealogies and Family
Histories: Chinese Geneaologies As Local
and Family History." In, *Heritage, Vol. II:
Asian and African and Local History.* Salt
Lake City, Utah: Church of Jesus Christ of
Latter Day Saints.

Heizer, Robert F., and Alan F. Almquist
1971   THE   OTHER CALIFORNIANS:
PREJUDICE AND DISCRIMINATION
UNDER SPAIN, MEXICO AND THE
UNITED STATES TO 1920. Berkeley:
University of California Press.

Hibbert, Christopher
>   1970   THE DRAGON WAKES: CHINA AND
>   THE WEST, 1793-1911. New York: Harper
>   & Row.

Hicks, John D.
>   1937   THE AMERICAN NATION. A HISTORY
>   OF THE UNITED STATES FROM 1865 TO
>   THE PRESENT. New York: Houghton
>   Mifflin Company.

Hoexter, Corinne
>   1976   FROM CANTON TO CALIFORNIA: THE
>   EPIC OF CHINESE IMMIGRATION. New
>   York: Four Winds Press.

Hong, Yon Chang
>   1925   Chinese Immigration. Thesis, University of
>   Southern California, School of Law.

Hooks, Brian
>   1982   THE CAMBRIDGE ENCYCLOPEDIA OF
>   CHINA. London: Cambridge University
>   Press.

Howell, Harry T.
>   1938   Operators Report on Camp Carson. M.S.
>   on file, La Grande Ranger District.

Hoy, William
>   1942   THE CHINESE SIX COMPANYS. San
>   Francisco (1,000 copies printed for the

Chinese Consolidated Benevolent
Association).

Hoyt, Edwin P.
1974 ASIANS IN THE WEST. New York:
Thomas Nelson Inc., Publishers.

Hsieh, Chiao-Min
1973 ATLAS OF CHINA. New York:
McGraw-Hill Book Company.

Hsu, Francis L. K.
1971 THE CHALLENGE OF THE AMERICAN
DREAM: THE CHINESE IN THE UNITED
STATES. Belmont, California: Wadsworth
Publishing Company, Inc.

Hudson, Lorelea
1978 Cultural Resource Overview of the
Malheur, Umatilla, and Wallowa-Whitman
National Forests, Northeast Oregon/
Southwest Washington. John Day, Oregon:
Malheur National Forest.

Hug, Bernal
n. d. HISTORY OF ELGIN, OREGON.
1961 HISTORY OF UNION COUNTY,
OREGON. (Ed.) Historical Society of
Union County: La Grande, Oregon.

Idaho Signal, Lewiston, Idaho
16 November 1972

Jackson, W. Turrentine
1985 "Portland: Wells Fargo's Hub for the Pacific Northwest." *Oregon Historical Quarterly*, V. LXXXVI, N. 3 (Fall, 1985), pp. 229-268.

Jaehnig, Manfred E., and Cynthia L. DeFries
1987 Historical Overview and Photographic Documentation Of The Hogum and Sparta Placer Mining Ditches. Wallowa-Whitman National Forest, Baker OR.

Jasper, Frank M.
1971 "The Chinese In Union County." In, *1960 Annual of the Union County Historical Society*, 2nd printing (B. Hug, ed.), pp. 5-25. La Grande, Oregon: KenRay Enterprises, Inc.

Jones, Timothy W.
1980 "Anthropological Test Excavations in the Boise Redevelopment Project Area, Boise, Idaho." *University of Idaho Anthropological Research Manuscript, No. 59.*

Jones, Timothy W., Mary Anne David, George Ling
1979 "Idaho City: An Overview and Report on Excavation." *University of Idaho Anthropological Research Manuscript Series*, No. 50. Moscow, Idaho: University of Idaho Press.

Klubischy, Tibor
　　　n.d.　　Report on Camp Carson Gold Placer Holdings Situated in Union Country. Report on file, La Grande Ranger District.

Knapp, Ronald G.
　　　1986　CHINA'S TRADITIONAL RURAL ARCHITECTURE: A CULTURAL GEOGRAPHY OF THE COMMON HOUSE. Honolulu: University of Hawaii Press.

Knoll, Tricia
　　　1982　BECOMING AMERICANS. ASIAN SOJOURNERS, IMMIGRANTS, AND REFUGES IN THE WESTERN UNITED STATES. Portland OR: Coast to Coast Books.

La Grande Gazette, Oregon
　　　9 March 1894.
　　　1 November 1895.

La Grande Observer, Oregon
　　　14 May 1938
　　　12 October 1938
　　　30 March 1939

Lai, H.M, and P.P. Choy
　　　1971　Outlines. History of the Chinese In America. Published by the Authors 1972; Chinese American Studies Planning Group, San Francisco Chinatown 1973.

LaLande, Jeffrey Max

    1981   Sojourners in the Oregon Siskiyous: Adaptation and Acculturation of the Chinese Miners in the Applegate Valley, ca. 1855-1900. Unpublished Masters Thesis, Oregon State University, Corvallis, Oregon.

    1983   "Hydraulic Mining Techniques of the Chinese in Southwestern Oregon: A Case of Technological Acculturation." Paper presented at the symposium: Chinese Historical Archaeology: Studies in Adaptation and Cultural Stability, 16th Annual Meeting of the Society for Historical Archaeology, Denver, January 7, 1983.

Lang, Olga

    1968   CHINESE FAMILY AND SOCIETY. Archon Press (reprint of Yale University Press, 1946).

Ling, George Kai Hung

    1980   A Content Analysis Of Chinese Crimes in Boise and Idaho City between 1865-1895. M.A. Thesis (Sociology), University of Idaho.

Ling, Pyau

    1912   "Causes of Chinese Immigration." *The Annals of the American Academy*, XXXIX (Jan 1912).

Lung, David Ping-Yee
    1978   Heaven, Earth and Man: Concepts and Processes Of Chinese Architecture and City Planning. Unpublished M. A. Thesis, Department of Architecture, University of Oregon, Eugene, Oregon.

Lyman, Horace S.
    1903   HISTORY OF OREGON: THE GROWTH OF AN AMERICAN STATE, Vol. 4. New York: Pacific Publishing Co.

Lyman, Stanford M.
    1970   THE ASIAN IN THE WEST. Reno, Nevada: Social Sciences & Humanities Publication No. 4, Western Studies Center, Desert Research Institute, University of Nevada.

Ma, L. Eve Armentrout
    1991   "Chinese in Marin County, 1850-1950: A Century of Growth and Decline." In, *Chinese America: History and Perspectives*, pp.25-48. San Francisco: Chinese Historical Society of America.

McArthur, Lewis A.
    1974   OREGON GEOGRAPHIC NAMES, 4th Edition. Portland OR: Oregon Historical Society.

McCunn, Ruthanne Lum
    1979   AN ILLUSTRATED HISTORY OF THE

CHINESE IN AMERICA. Design Enterprises of San Francisco.

March, Andrew L.
1968 "An Apprecation of Chinese Geomancy." *Journal of Asian Studies*, V. 27, N. 2, pp. 253-267.

Mead, George R.
1974 Growth in the Grande Ronde Valley, Oregon, 1862-1865: Roadways, Stagecoach Lines, and Settlement. Unpublished m.s. on file, La Grande Ranger District, and copy in author's possession.
1992 Chinese in the U. S. Census: 1860, 1870, 1880, 1900. Unpublished m.s. in author's possession.
2006 A HISTORY OF UNION COUNTY. La Grande, Oregon: E-Cat worlds.

Morning Observer, La Grande, Oregon
9 August 1903.
15 August 1903.

Morrison, Larry
n.d. An Essay On The Natural History of the Southernmost Portion of The Wallowa Mountains. Thesis for Masters Degree - Education, Eastern Oregon State College, La Grande, OR.

Mountain Sentinel, La Grande, Oregon
1 August 1868.

24 October 1868.

19 October 1872.

12 September 1874.

20 June 1875.

20 November 1875.

23 December 1876.

29 March 1895.

Meyers, Danielle D.
    1998   Guest of the Gold Mountain: Chinese
            Vernacular Architecture and Two Dragon
            Camp. Senior Thesis. Western Oregon
            University.

Nee, Victor G., and Brett de Nary Nee
    1972   LONGTIME   CALIFORN':   A
            DOCUMENTARY STORY OF AN
            AMERICAN CHINATOWN. New York:
            Pantheon Books.

Newsom, E. Earl
    1972   DAVID NEWSOM: THE WESTERN
            OBSERVER 1805-1882. Portland OR:
            Oregon Historical Society.

Nokes, R. Gregory
    2009   MASSACRED FOR GOLD. THE CHINESE
            IN HELLS CANYON. Corvallis: Oregon
            State University Press.

Norton, Henry K.
    1924   THE STORY OF CALIFORNIA FROM
            THE EARLIEST DAYS TO THE PRESENT,

7th ed. Chicago: A.C. McClurg & Co.

Observer, The, La Grande, Oregon
24 September 1940.

Oliphant, J. Orin
1968   ON THE CATTLE RANGES OF THE
OREGON COUNTRY. Seattle: University
of Washington Press.

Oliver, Mrs. Turner
1927   Letter to L.M. Duncan. Copy of file, La
Grande Ranger District.

Oregonian
1868   August 8.

Ohai, Jean
1980   "Family History For Chinese Americans."
In, WORLD CONFERENCE ON
RECORDS: PRESERVING OUR
HERITAGE, VOL. II: ASIAN AND
AFRICAN FAMILY AND LOCAL
HISTORY. Salt Lake City: Church of Jesus
Christ of Latter-Day Saints.

Olsen, John W.
1978   "A Study of Chinese Ceramics Excavated
in Tucson." *The Kiva*, 44(1). Tucson,
Arizona.

Ong, Paul
    1983   "Chinese Laundries as an Urban Occupation." Seattle WA: The Annuals of the Chinese Historical Society of the Pacific Northwest.

Ow, Yuk, Him Mark Lai and Phillip P. Choy
    1973   OUTLINES: HISTORY OF THE CHINESE IN AMERICA. San Francisco: ChineseAmerican Studies Planning Group, San Francisco Chinatown.

Palmer, Spencer J. (Ed.)
    1972   STUDIES IN ASIAN GENEALOGY. Provo: Brigham University Press.

Parsons, Colonel William
    1902   AN ILLUSTRATED HISTORY OF UMATILLA COUNTY. W. H. Lever, Publisher.

Paul, Rodman Wilson
    1938   "The Origin of the Chinese Issue in California." *The Mississippi Valley Historical Review*, Vol. 25, No. 2, Sept 1938.
    1970   "The Origin of the Chinese Issue in California." In, *The Aliens: A History of Ethnic Minorities in America*, pp. 161-172. New York: Appleton-Century-Crofts.
    1974   MINING FRONTIERS OF THE FAR WEST, 1848-1880. University of New Mexico Press.

1982 "After the Gold Rush: San Francisco and Portland." *Pacific Historical Review*, No. 1 (Feb), pp 1-21.

Pfaelzer, Jean
2008 DRIVEN OUT. THE FORGOTTEN WAR AGAINST CHINESE AMERICANS. Berkeley: University of California Press.

Pirazzoli-T'Serstevens, Michèle
1971 LIVING ARCHITECTURE: CHINESE (English translation: Robert Allen). New York: Grosset & Dunlap, Inc

Rand, Helen B.
1974 GOLD, JADE AND ELEGANCE. Baker, Oregon: The Record-Courier, Printers.

Raymond, Rossiter W.
1873 STATISTICS OF MINES AND MINING IN THE STATES AND TERRITORIES WEST OF THE ROCKY MOUNTAINS. FIFTH ANNUAL REPORT, UNITED STATE COMMISSIONER OF MINING STATISTICS. 42ND CONGRESS, 3RD SESSION, HOUSE OF REPRESENTATIVES, EX. DOC. NO. 210. Washington D.C.: Government Printing Office.

Remy, F.W.
1928 Report on Camp Carson Gold Placer Holdings Situated in Union County.

Report of file, La Grande Ranger District.

Ritchie, Neville
1980 "The Excavation of A Nineteenth Century Chinese Mining Settlement at Cromwell, Central Otago." *New Zealand Archaeological Association Newsletter,* Vol. 23 (2), pp. 69-82.
1981 "Archaeological Interpretation of Alluvial Gold Tailing Sites, Central Otago, New Zealand." *New Zealand Journal of Archaeology,* Vol. 3, pp 51-69.
1986 Archaeology and History of the Chinese in Southern New Zealand during the Nineteenth Century: A Study of Acculturation, Adaptation, and Change. Ph.D. Dissertation, Anthropology Department, University of Otago, Dunedin, New Zealand.

Rohe, Randall E.
1982 "After the Gold Rush. Chinese Mining in The Far West, 1850-1890." *Montana The Magazine of Western History* (Autumn). Helena MT: Montana Historical Society.

Sandmeyer, Elmer Clarence
1973 THE ANTI-CHINESE MOVEMENT IN CALIFORNIA. Urbana: University of Illinois Press. (A reprint of the 1939 edition).

Saxton, Alexander

    1995   THE INDISPENSABLE ENEMY. LABOR AND THE ANTI-CHINESE MOVEMENT IN CALIFORNIA. Berkeley: University of California Press. (Reprint of 1971).

Shaw, William

    1973   GOLDEN DREAMS AND WAKING REALITIES. New York: ARNO Press (reprint of 1851 edition).

Shay, Frank (compiler)

    1876   Chinese Immigration: The Social, Moral and Political Effect. (Testimony taken before a committee of the Senate of the State of California). State Printing Office, Sacramento, California.

Simerville, Clara L.

    1986   ONE CENTURY OF LIFE: DUNHAM WRIGHT OF OREGON, 1842-1942. Corvallis, Oregon: Simerville.

Smith, Cortland L.

    1979   SALMON FISHERIES OF THE COLUMBIA. Corvallis, Oregon: Oregon State University Press.

Sowell, Thomas

    1996   MIGRATIONS AND CULTURES. A WORLD VIEW. New York: Basic Books.

Speer, William
    1870 THE OLDEST AND THE NEWEST EMPIRE. CHINA AND THE UNITED STATES. Hartford, Conn: S.S. Scranton and Company.

Spier, Robert F. G.
    1958a "Food Habits of Nineteenth-Century California Chinese." *California Historical Society Quarterly* (March), pp. 79-84.
    1958b "Tool Acculturation Among 19th-Century California Chinese." *Ethnohistory*, 5 (2), pp. 97-117.

Spreen, Christian August
    1939 A History of Placer Gold Mining In Oregon, 1850-1867. Masters Thesis - History. University of Oregon, Eugene OR.

Steele, R. F.
    1904 A HISTORY OF NORTHERN WASHINGTON. Spokane, Washington.

Steeves, Laban Richard
    1984 Chinese Gold Miners of Northeastern Oregon, 1862-1900. A thesis presented to the Interdisciplinary Studies Program: Historical Archaeology and Graduate School, University of Oregon.

Steiner, Stan
    1979   FUSANG. THE CHINESE WHO BUILT
            AMERICA. New York: Harper & Row,
            Publishers.

Stenger, Alison T.
    1992   "The Universal Overseas Site: A
            Predictable Ceramic Assemblage."
            *Supplement to Asian Comparative Collecvon
            Newsletter*, 9(1), March. Alfred W. Bowers
            Laboratory of Anthropology, University of
            Moscow, Idaho.

Sullivan, Daniel D.
    1983   "Archaeological Investigation of the China
            House at the Warrendale Cannery, 1876-
            1930." Paper present at the 16th Annual
            Meeting of the Society for Historical
            Archaeology, Denver, January 7, 1983.

Sung, Betty Lee
    1967   MOUNTAIN OF GOLD. THE STORY OF
            THE CHINESE IN AMERICA. New York:
            McMillan Company.

Sutter, Gen. John A.
    1857   "The Discovery of Gold in California."
            Hutching's California Magazine (November).

Swartout, Jr., Robert R.
    1982   "In Defense of The West's Chinese."
            Oregon Historical Quarterly (Spring), Vol.
            LXXXIII, No. 1, pp. 25-36.

Takaki, Ronald T.
>   1979   IRON CAGES: RACE AND CULTURE IN
>   NINETEETH-CENTURY AMERICA. New
>   York: Alfred A. Knopf.

Tucker, Gerald J.
>   1981   Historical Sketches of Wallowa National
>   Forest. M.S. On file, La Grande Ranger
>   District, Wallowa-Whitman National
>   Forest.

Trull, Fern Coble
>   1964   The History of the Chinese in Idaho.
>   Masters thesis, University of Oregon.

Tsai, Shih-Shan Henry
>   1970   Reaction To Exclusion: Ch'ing Attitudes
>   Towards Overseas Chinese in the United
>   States, 1848-1906. Unpublished Ph. D.
>   Dissertation, University of Oregon,
>   Eugene, Oregon.
>   1986   THE CHINESE EXPERIENCE IN
>   AMERICA. Bloomington, Indiana: Indiana
>   University Press.

Tuan, Yi-Fu
>   1974   TOPOPHILIA: A STUDY OF
>   ENVIRONMENTAL PERCEPTION,
>   ATTITUDES, AND VALUES. Englewood
>   Cliffs, New Jersey: Prentice-Hall, Inc.

Uchida, Naosaku
>   1960   The Oversea Chinese. A Bibliographical
>   Essay Based on the Resources of the

Hoover Institution. *Hoover Institution, Bibliographical Series VII.* Hoover Institution On War, Revolution, and Peace. Stanford University.

Union County Courthouse Records, La Grande OR
Court Case No. 488, August 1871
Book A, Deeds
Book A, Mortgages
Quartz Records - Books D, E, G, H, I.
Mining Deeds - Books B, C, D, E.
Placer Records - Books B, C.
Mining Records - Books A, B, 1.

Walling, A. G.
1884 HISTORY OF SOUTHERN OREGON. Portland, Oregon: A. G. Walling Printing Company,

Walters, Derek
1988 FENG SHUI: PERFECT PLACING FOR YOUR HAPPINESS AND PROSPERITY. New York: Pagoda Books.

Waley, Arthur (translator, annotator)
1989 THE ANALECTS OF CONFUCIUS. New York: Vintage Books.

Washington Statesmen
8 February 1867

Weekly Oregonian
1 October 1857

Weekly Republican, La Grande, Oregon
　　12 September 1896.
　　14 November 1896.

WHPC (Western Historical Publishing Company)
　　1902a AN ILLUSTRATED HISTORY OF BAKER,
　　　　　GRANT, MALHEUR, AND HARNEY
　　　　　COUNTIES. Western Historical Publishing
　　　　　Company, Inc.
　　1902b AN ILLUSTRATED HISTORY OF UNION
　　　　　AND WALLOWA COUNTIES. Western
　　　　　Historical Publishing Company, Inc.

Williams, Stephen
　　1930 THE CHINESE IN THE CALIFORNIA
　　　　　MINES, 1848-1860. R and E Research
　　　　　Associates, San Francisco, California.
　　　　　(Reprinted in 1971).

Willson, Margaret, and Jeffery L. MacDonald
　　1983 "Racial Tension At Port Townsend and
　　　　　Bellingham Bay: 1870-1886." Seattle WA:
　　　　　The Annuals of The Chinese Historical
　　　　　Society of the Pacific Northwest.

Winther, Oscar Osburn
　　1949 THE GREAT NORTHWEST: A HISTORY.
　　　　　Alfred A. Knopf: New York.
　　1950 THE OLD OREGON COUNTRY: A
　　　　　HISTORY OF FRONTIER TRAVEL,
　　　　　TRANSPORTATION, AND TRAVEL.
　　　　　Stanford University Press.

Woods, Daniel B.
1851   SIXTEEN MONTH'S AT THE GOLD DIGGINGS. New York: ARNO Press (reprinted in 1973).

Wynn, Robert Edward
1964   REACTION TO THE CHINESE IN THE PACIFIC NORTHWEST AND BRITISH COLUMBIA, 1850 TO 1910. Ph. D. Dissertation, University of Washington, Seattle, Washington. (Published by ARNO Press, 1978).

Yu, Li-hua
1991   Chinese Immigrants in Idaho. Ph.D. dissertation, Bowling Green State University.

Yutang, Lin
1939   MY COUNTRY AND MY PEOPLE. New York: The John Day Company.

Zhu, Liping
1997   A CHINAMAN'S CHANCE. THE CHINESE ON THE ROCKY MOUNTAIN MINING FRONTIER. Boulder, CO: University of Colorado press.

About the Author

George R. Mead began to study anthropology in 1962 after being discharged (honorably) from the U. S. Army, Combat Engineers. He eventually received his degrees, a B.A., a M.A., and a Ph.D. in his chosen field. And many years later an M. S. W. in Clinical Social Work. He has worked in aerospace, taught at the college and university levels, worked in a community action agency, ran a restaurant, been unemployed, and worked for the U. S. Forest Service. He is now retired from the work-a-day world but does a certain amount of consulting, writing, and research. He lives seven miles outside of the small town of La Grande, Oregon, with his wife, one cat. A new dog joined the house as an eight-week old puppy found by the German Shepard Katy (now deceased) under some brush in the middle of the American Southwest desert. Rez now weighs 100 pounds (some puppy).

www.ingramcontent.com/pod-product-compliance
Lightning Source LLC
Chambersburg PA
CBHW072133270326
41931CB00010B/1744